Being Methodist
in the Bible Belt

Being Methodist in the Bible Belt

A THEOLOGICAL SURVIVAL GUIDE FOR YOUTH, PARENTS, AND OTHER CONFUSED METHODISTS

F. Belton Joyner Jr.

Westminster John Knox Press
LOUISVILLE • LONDON

Scripture quotations from the New Revised Standard Version of the Bible are copyright © 1989 by the Division of Christian Education of the National Council of the Churches of Christ in the U.S.A. and are used by permission.

Book design and cover design by RohaniDesign.com

First edition
Published by Westminster John Knox Press
Louisville, Kentucky

This book is printed on acid-free paper that meets the American National Standards Institute Z39.48 standard. ⊗

PRINTED IN THE UNITED STATES OF AMERICA

04 05 06 07 08 09 10 11 12 13 — 10 9 8 7 6 5 4 3 2 1

Library of Congress Cataloging-in-Publication Data

Joyner, F. Belton
    Being Methodist in the Bible Belt : a theological survival guide for youth, parents, and other confused Methodists / F. Belton Joyner, Jr. — 1st ed.
       p. cm
    Includes bibliographical references (p.).
    ISBN 0-664-22685-X (alk. paper)
    1. United Methodist Church (U.S.)—Doctrines. I. Title.

BX8382.2.Z5J69 2004
287'.6—dc22

                                                          2003064502

To
Belton IV, Vance, and Grady
growing in grace

Contents

Introduction

When I first started working on these pages, I decided that I would use bumper stickers as a way of presenting the various issues to be explored. I saw a sticker that said, "The Bible says it; I believe it; that settles it!" Now, that would a perfect introduction to talking about Scripture as primary for Methodist thought. Then, a car in a hospital parking lot offered this message: "My mother is the tour guide on a guilt trip." Perfect! This claim opens the door to conversation about sin and forgiveness and families and all sorts of things about which we should think.

> My mother is the tour guide on a guilt trip.

Then there are all those signs on the backs of cars depicting fish eating fish. I must confess that I have never quite been able to sort out who believes what with those emblems (something about Darwin and evolution), but I figured those fish would be a good place to start looking at science and faith, creation and religion. (After all, the earliest Christians used the fish as a sign for believers because the Greek word for fish—*ichthus*—formed an acronym for the Greek for Jesus Christ, Son of God, Savior of the World.)

I was on a roll. Bumper stickers would be the glue to hold together this book. At least that is what I thought, until I was on Interstate 85 driving a very respectable 64 miles per hour in a 65 mph zone. (Okay, I want to honest throughout this book, so I'll admit it: I was going 70 miles per hour. They give you five miles per hour, don't they?) In front of me was a red BMW, and on the rear bumper was a sticker, just waiting to be read. When I got close enough to see that it said something about Jesus, I knew I had to read the rest of it. (You see, I was doing research on behalf of you, dear reader.)

I was now going 72, 73, 75 miles per hour, gaining on the car that held the mystery message about our Lord. In fact, I gained so much that I put my Toyota within a nose length of the BMW bumper. Suddenly, the BMW sped up considerably, as did my imagination: the occupants of the car would go up ahead three or four miles and then pull over and wait until I passed by. Then they would force me to stop and seek various ways to rearrange my body. Their anger over my tailgating would turn into a claim on my medical insurance (where was the nearest hospital where I could be put back together?).

None of that happened. The red sedan simply disappeared. I never found out what that bumper sticker said, but I did decide that perhaps bumper stickers would not be the way to establish the themes of this book.

How then shall we go about it? This book is theology. (Steady now! *Theology* means "expressions about God," so this book is about ways that various folk think and feel about God.) In particular, these chapters explore how Methodists think and feel about God. (I have checked the small print; nothing says that only Methodists can read this!)

Methodists are part of the Christian Church family that grows out of a religious revival in England in the eighteenth century. The names most often associated with the start of the movement that became Methodism are John Wesley and his brother Charles. In the United States, a central beginning figure was Francis Asbury. Most Methodists can find at least one church named "Wesley Memorial Church" or "Asbury Church." (For that matter, most Methodists can find a congregation named "First Church," but I do not know anything about John First, Charles First, or Francis First, so I guess that is another story. Speaking of First, did you hear about the person who said he would not go to see Shakespeare's *Henry V* because he was tired of films that were sequels?)

Methodists are a mixed lot. There are British Methodists, African Methodist Episcopal Methodists (AME), and Christian Methodist Episcopal Methodists (CME). Then there are African Methodist Episcopal Zion Methodists (AMEZ). There are also Wesleyan Methodists, Free Methodists, Evangelical Methodists, and United Methodists. That's where

I fit in. I am a United Methodist. That reality becomes the lens through which I look at things. It includes the heritage of the Evangelical United Brethren Church and the roots of the Methodist Church. Those two groups merged in 1968 to form The United Methodist Church (UMC).

So where does that leave us? I cannot even pretend to speak for all the United Methodists in the world, much less for the millions and millions who are in other branches of the Methodist tree. On what kind of theology—thinking about God—can so many people agree? (I don't even agree with everything that is said in the Lizzie Grey Chandler Sunday School class I attend at Bethany Church; how can I match up with umpteen million other folks?)

How then shall we go about establishing our themes? Well, for starters, United Methodists do have some standards for our teaching (our doctrine). But, truth to tell, folks who like to stay up late at night worrying about this kind of thing do not agree on what those standards are.

A SIDE TRIP FOR A LITTLE BACKGROUND

Every four years, about one thousand United Methodists from around the world come together to set a direction for the denomination and to enact any legislation needed to help the mission of the Church "to make disciples of Jesus Christ."[1] These persons—an equal number of clergy and laypersons—have been elected from each region where the United Methodist Church is organized. This body is called the General Conference.

The General Conference adopts *The Book of Discipline,* a volume containing everything you ever wanted to know about Methodism (and probably several things you did not want to know!). It contains historical statements, theological statements, social justice statements, and a ton of stuff about how the United Methodist experience ought to be organized and lived.[2]

The Constitution of The United Methodist Church is in *The Book of Discipline.* It lists six things the General Conference cannot do (called "Restrictive Rules"). Changing any of these restrictions takes a two-thirds vote of the General Conference and two-thirds vote of all the members of the annual (regional) conferences, except—and this exception lets you know that this is of big-time importance—for two of the restrictions, which could be changed only if three-fourths of the members of the annual conferences voted to do so.

What are these two rules?

Article 1 of the restrictive rules says, "The General Conference shall not revoke, alter, or change our Articles of Religion or establish any new standards or rules of doctrine contrary to our present existing and established standards of doctrine." Article 2 indicates that "The General Conference shall not revoke, alter, or change our Confession of Faith."[3] (Remember that The United Methodist Church was formed from two denominations: article 1 comes from The Methodist Church; article 2 comes from the Evangelical United Brethren Church.)

So, to determine what United Methodists teach, all we have to do is to find "our present existing and established standards of doctrine." Gasp and sputter! Present when? Existing when? Established by whom? Standards for whom? Where is John Wesley when you need him?!

Students of Methodist thought do not agree on what constitute these established standards of doctrine. (You are reading this book, so count yourself a student of Methodist thought. Congratulations.) The possibilities include the Articles of Religion, John Wesley's *Explanatory Notes upon the New Testament*, the Confession of Faith, and The *Standard Sermons* of John Wesley (either 44 or 51 or 53 of them, depending on how you are counting).

A SIDE TRIP FOR A LITTLE BACKGROUND

John Wesley lived from 1703 to 1791. A priest in the Church of England, he was the central figure in a religious revival in England. When the movement spread to the American colonies, it slowly began some separation from its English roots. (Remember, this was in the midst of the American Revolution.) In 1784, the movement organized as the Methodist Episcopal Church in America, distinct from its mother, the Church of England.

Mr. Wesley continued to play an influential role. He adapted the Articles of Religion (statements of belief) of the Church of England for use in the United States. As early as 1813, predecessors of the Evangelical United Brethren Church established a Confession of Faith (statements of belief). Methodist theologians agree that the Articles of Religion and the Confession of Faith are appropriate standards of doctrine.

The fuss comes over the *Sermons* and the *Explanatory Notes upon the New Testament*. Are they merely important guidelines or do they have legal standing? Are they simply useful tools for Methodist theology or do they carry a special authority? The answer to each of these questions seems to be "Yes."[4]

John Wesley usually preached without notes. The collection of *Standard Sermons* is a gathering of his teaching material put into sermon form. It is not likely that he often preached "word for word" from these written texts. Nevertheless, he often preached several times a day, frequently outdoors when he was denied access to regular pulpits. Mr. Wesley offered the collection of his sermons as a way of measuring the teaching of those who wanted to be in connection with him. (He called the Methodist movement "the connexion.") He expected "his preachers" to make the same emphases that he did.

Methodist teaching was rooted solidly and unashamedly in the Bible. To help persons draw the plain truth from the Scripture, Mr. Wesley developed *Explanatory Notes upon the New Testament*. (He also prepared a similar work for the Old Testament, but most of it was directly chosen from other writers.) The *Explanatory Notes* gave guidelines for interpreting the biblical text and allowed Mr. Wesley a setting for offering his distinctive insights into the written Word of God.

The debate among Methodist thinkers over which documents to use as the doctrinal standards is somewhat beyond the range of this book. (Although it is not the focus of my writing, it is a necessary discussion for the Church. "Dissemination of doctrines contrary to the established standards of doctrines of The United Methodist Church" is one of the charges against clergy or laypeople that can lead to church trial and the possibility of loss of clergy credentials or the loss of membership in the United Methodist Church.)[5]

How then shall we go about it? How shall we put the Methodist journey into conversation with today's cultural religion? What help is there for a young Methodist (young in years or otherwise fresh on the trail) who is confronted with other Christians who talk a different kind of talk? How can you and I be in conversation as I sit out in the country near Bahama, North Carolina, and you sit there in (fill in the blank)? How shall we bring about world peace and a secure economic future for all peoples? (Oh, well—that last one is not up for grabs here, but I figured that as long as I was asking tough questions, I might as well throw that one in too.)

Let's try it this way. I'll pick some ingredients that are essential to Methodist life. (Remember, as I pick these up, my hands are wrapped in United Methodist gloves.) I'll ponder out loud—okay, in print—about these components of the Methodist theological journey (the way Methodists speak about God). Along the way, I'll point out some ways "Methodist-speak" is different from what others in the twenty-first century are saying, even other Christians. (I'll try to be fair to others, but the truth is that the sin of stereotyping is usually easier than the discipline of fairness.) If Methodists do not agree, I'll work to say so (but you understand that my version of the truth is a pure, unalloyed, direct revelation—sort of!).

Your job is to enjoy all this. My guess is that you will enjoy it most by being open in heart and mind and by growing in your own faith response. My guess is that you will enjoy it most by joining in the dialogue.

From time to time, you will come across the heading "What Are You Going to Do About It?" That will be a flag inviting you to slow down for a moment, to reflect on what you have been reading, and, in good Methodist fashion, to do something about it.

A SIDE TRIP FOR A LITTLE BACKGROUND

You know the classic answer to the question "Why did the chicken cross the road?" (To get to the other side). Do you know why the chicken went half way across the road? (She wanted to lay it on the line.) Do you know why the chicken went back and forth, back and forth, crossing the road over and over again? (She wanted to show the possum that it could be done! Around here, we say "possum" because that is the animal we most often find dead by the side of the road. If that doesn't work for you, substitute armadillo or snake or moose, or whatever works for your part of the country. Come to think of it, you probably should not try this with a moose.)

"She wanted to show the possum that it could be done!" In some ways, that illustrates a Methodist approach to life. It is the doing that is at the heart of the Christian life. If you ask some folks to tell you about their congregation, they will begin, "Here is what we believe . . ." and then they will tell you three or four core beliefs. If you ask a Methodist to tell you about his or her church, more likely you will get a recital of what the congregation does: "Well, we go on mission trips; we have lots of Bible study groups; we have two services of worship; we have a wonderful youth group."

Those "doings" of course grow directly out of what is believed, but Methodists tend to think it's not worth believing if it doesn't make a difference in what you do.

And here is a word about the title of this book, *Being Methodist in the Bible Belt*. The truth is that someone else came up with that title. (I thought this volume might be called *Prolegomenon to a Careful and Reasoned Reflection on the Encounter of United Methodism with the Religious Values of the Twenty-first Century*. Rather catchy, don't you think?)

It's the "Bible Belt" part that gives a bit of pause. Exactly where is that . . . or what is that . . . or, maybe, who is that? It's nowhere and it's everywhere. It's a belt like a corn belt, not a belt like a pants-holder-upper. The Corn Belt is a swath of the country in which corn is a major agricultural product. The Bible Belt is that portion of our culture in which the Bible not only holds a traditional place of high attention but is often interpreted in a fairly restrictive fashion. It is no particular place; it's more of a mind-set, a way of looking at life.

The Bible Belt represents a particular way of looking at the Bible (sometimes accompanied by a conviction that everyone else's way of looking at the Bible is wrong). Bible Belt thought often takes the Bible as being literally true. Methodists tend to feel it is more important to take the Bible seriously than it is to take the Bible literally. The Bible Belt may look at the Bible in a microcosmic way (like through a microscope, finding small, isolated bits of information); Methodists are more likely to look at the Bible in a macrocosmic way (looking for the big picture, the overall message).

Sometimes the Bible Belt attitude and the Methodist approach share the same vocabulary (but with different meanings): salvation, hell, kingdom. Sometimes the Bible Belt gives emphases that are missing in Methodism: rapture,[6] dispensation, inerrancy. Sometimes Methodism underlines themes that are weakened or missing from the Bible Belt: social justice, ecumenism.

It is tempting to make fun of those with whom we disagree (particularly if they think I am going to hell for disagreeing). Alas, I often judge others at their worst and expect them to judge me at my best. In these pages, I hope to be fair, but I want to tell the whole story—of course, the story from the point of view of a United Methodist!

A SIDE TRIP FOR A LITTLE BACKGROUND

James went off to college. When he had been away for about two weeks, he called home.

"How are things going?" he asked his younger brother.

"Okay. Nothing much happening."

"How's Cleo?" James inquired.

"Oh, yeah," his brother said. "She's dead."

James was aghast. He had loved that cat ever since he'd found her as a scrawny kitten. He had nursed Cleo back to health and even let her sleep in his bed. "That's terrible! And what an awful way to tell me! You know how much that cat meant to me!"

His brother mumbled, "Well, how was I supposed to tell you?"

James took a deep breath and tried to be patient. "You could have broken the news to me gradually, gently. For example, when I called you could have said something like 'Cleo is up on the roof and we can't get her to come down.' I would have worried about that but not too much. The next time I called you could say, 'Cleo is getting skinny and looks kind of weak.' Naturally, this would bother me, but would not be such a shock. When I called the next time, you could say, 'We finally got Cleo to the vet and the doc says things don't look too good.' Then, at least when I called the next time, I'd be prepared to hear such dreadful news as 'Poor Cleo has passed away.'"

"Okay," said the little brother. "I'll try to do better next time."

About a month later, James called home again. His little brother answered the phone.

"How are things going?"

"Okay. Not much happening."

"And how is Mom?" asked James.

There was a pause. "Uh, she's up on the roof and we can't get her to come down."

There is more than one way to tell the whole story. This book is about hearing a Methodist voice tell the story.

What Are You Going to Do About It?

1. If you are reading this book alone, find someone who will share the journey with you. The sparks might be a bit brighter if you find someone who is likely to disagree with you, or with Methodism, or, heavens forbid, with me.
2. Start a journal of questions and issues you want to explore more deeply. (Maybe you could use the attractive blank margins of this book or the space at the end of each chapter for your scribbling.) Who is someone whose faith walk is such that you would find their insights useful?
3. Think of someone whose religion makes you nervous. Pray that God might grant you grace to learn from that person and grace to offer that person the gifts of your own faith.

1

The House

About thirty miles from where I live is a church with a gigantic message board. The sign area is one of those biggies with interchangeable letters. One week the words might be "Welcome"; another time the same space might say, "Revival Tonight at 7:00." Usually, the statement is along these lines: "17 saved last week" or "10 saved last week" or "21 saved last week."

Keeping score of what God has done is one way of declaring and celebrating the power of God. (Check out Acts 1:15; 2:47; 4:4, for example.) Nevertheless, even without seeing an

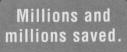

Millions and millions saved.

identification marker, one could be pretty sure the church I mentioned above is not a Methodist congregation. Certainly, it is not because Methodists do not care about salvation. Indeed, it is because Methodists care so deeply about salvation that such a billboard claim does not represent full Methodist thought.

A SIDE TRIP FOR A LITTLE BACKGROUND

"Getting saved" is *de rigueur* in Bible Belt culture: socially expected and a rite of passage. In fact, one can apparently get "extra points" by being able to name the time and place of salvation.

> Methodists seem to appreciate both the story of the dramatic conversion of Saul (Acts 9:3–19) and the account of Timothy, who was evidently nurtured slowly into faith (2 Tim. 1:5). Some Methodists report how quickly and how sweepingly God rescued them from sin ("My life was filled with the devil; I tried to live without Jesus; I did not know how much God loved me, but then one night. . . ."). Other Methodists say that they cannot remember a time when they did not realize that God loved them ("I grew up in a Christian home and always felt accepted by God; faith was given to me before I knew it."). And Methodists enjoy claiming that both of these types of folks have been saved! No wonder most Methodist churches would not put up a sign indicating how many were saved last week because that would tell only part of the story. The common feature of both of these kinds of experiences is that God was the initiator; God was the starter. Salvation is really a story about what God has done more than it is a story about what we have done. For a Methodist, a good answer to the question "When were you saved?" might be "In A.D. 29 when Jesus died and rose from the dead." It is what God has done in Jesus Christ that defines salvation. Maybe it is looking at two sides of the same coin: in Bible Belt mentality, the question is "When did you say 'yes' to God?" In Methodist mentality, the question is "When did God say 'yes' to you?"

John Wesley taught that coming to faith is not the goal of the religious journey. It is important. It is critical. It is necessary. But it is not the goal. In the Wesleyan tradition, the end of the road is not an altar where one has knelt in deep repentance and accepted Jesus Christ as Lord and Savior. Hooray when that happens—but it is not the end of the road.

Mr. Wesley often got into extended written battles about theology. When he wrote something in a published leaflet, it was like posting it on an Internet bulletin board. All kinds of people got into the conversation. (Today, most of the impassioned message boards seem to be about sports teams. I must admit, it does get the blood stirring to read what some anonymous person has written negatively about my favorite teams. How dare he or she insult the Duke

Blue Devils! How dreadful that someone would denounce the St. Louis Cardinals! How could anyone even think of something bad to say about the Carolina Hurricanes, or the Charlotte Bobcats, or the Carolina Panthers!)

When Wesley tried to state clearly the Methodist understanding of a matter, other folks would tear into him. One such case occurred when John Wesley penned "The Principles of a Methodist Farther Explained." Thomas Church fired back an answer. (Mr. Church wins the contest for best title, or at least longest; he called his article "Some Farther Remarks on the Rev. Mr. John Wesley's Last Journal, together with a few considerations on his Farther Appeal; showing the inconsistency of his Conduct and Sentiments with the Constitution and Doctrine of the Church of England, and explaining the Articles relating to Justification, to which is annexed a Vindication of the Remarks, being a Reply to Mr. Wesley's answer, in a second Letter to that Gentleman, by Thomas Church, A.M., Vicar of Battlesea, and Prebendary of St. Paul's.")

In Mr. Wesley's reply to Mr. Church's reply to Mr. Wesley's reply to Mr. Church's remarks (!), John Wesley wrote, "Our main doctrines, which include all the rest, are three, that of repentance, of faith, and of holiness. The first of these we account, as it were, the porch of religion; the next, the door; the third is religion itself."[1]

Salvation is like a house. To get into the house, you have to first get on the porch (repentance) and then you have to go through the door (faith). But the house itself—one's relationship with God—is holiness, holy living.

A SIDE TRIP FOR A LITTLE BACKGROUND

Jan was a junior at Mebane High School and for months had looked forward to the class spring trip to the beach. Three car washes and four bake sales later, the funds were in hand and the bus was filled with classmates and counselors, eager for the first splash of the ocean, the first whiff of salt air. It was a Mebane tradition: seniors went to New York; juniors went to the beach.

After checking into the hotel ("Now, remember—absolutely no girls on the second floor, absolutely no boys on the third floor!") the teens hit the sands. They had two hours before supper.

Jan had not intended to get away from the group ("Now, you must stick together! There should always be at least three of you in a group"). It wouldn't take long to go back to get the forgotten sun block, so rather than bothering anyone, Jan sprinted alone across the beach and jogged back to the hotel. Sun block secured, Jan started back.

Two young men—they appeared to be college age—were soon walking alongside Jan. Friendly enough, they asked, "Just get here? The weather is going to be great this weekend!" Jan nodded and kept moving. "Can we ask you a question?" they continued, "an important question?" Jan, now wishing that a few other classmates were around, said, "I suppose so."

The taller of the two fellows said, "If you died tonight, would you go to heaven?"

The other companion spoke before Jan could answer. "It's simple. Admit you are a sinner and ask Jesus to save you. That's all there is to it."

The waves gave a rhythmic background to the conversation, but instead of the splash of sea water, all Jan could hear was an echo in her ears: "That's all there is to it."

Methodists care a lot about repentance. (There are 24 hymns in the *United Methodist Hymnal* in the section on invitation and repentance.) Methodists care a lot about asking Jesus to pardon our sin. (There are 21 hymns in the *United Methodist Hymnal* in the section on pardon and assurance of pardon.) But Methodists still understand what Mr. Wesley meant when he wrote that the house of religion was holiness, holy living. (There are 168 hymns in the *United Methodist Hymnal* in the section on holy living.)[2] Methodists would not agree with the two folks who stopped Jan at the beach: "That's all there is to it" leaves people stuck on the porch or lodged in the door. Repentance and faith (both possible by God's grace) are access to the house. The goal is not the porch or the door. The goal is the house itself.

One thing is clear. Repentance, faith, and holiness are all gifts of God's grace. Grace is God's preemptive strike on anything that would separate us from God. As Paul writes in his letter to the Romans, "Who will separate us from the love of Christ? Will hardship, or distress, or persecution, or famine, or nakedness, or peril, or sword? . . . No, in all these things we are more than conquerors through him who loved us. For I am convinced that neither death, nor life, nor angels, nor rulers, nor things present, nor things to come, nor powers, nor height, nor depth, nor anything else in all creation, will be able to separate us from the love of God in Christ Jesus" (Rom. 8:35; 37–39).

A SIDE TRIP FOR A LITTLE BACKGROUND

My family accuses me of eavesdropping. They are right. If I am standing in line at the airport, I listen to what others in the line are saying. (Often I hear, "Now be sure not to try and be funny when you get to security; they don't laugh.") If I am at a ball game, at half time, my attention moves from the game to whatever the folks behind me are discussing. ("Well, I said to her that if you are going to act like that I am not going to stand for it and you can just take your prissy self and get out of here" was one of the more interesting monologues.) Of course, I am not an audio-voyeur. I do this eavesdropping for professional reasons; I am a preacher and I am just trying to gain insights into the human condition (hmmm!), be available to help people (hmmm!), and to pick up a story I can use next Sunday (yeah!).

One night my wife and I were at a restaurant. When the waiter went to serve the next table, I could not help but hear (well, I did have to strain a little to hear clearly) as all eight people at the table declined the complimentary cup of coffee. "What are the odds of that?" I asked myself. Then, it dawned on me: Mormons! As they walked out the door, I heard them speak of a stake meeting, a term I recognized as a Mormon term. Indeed, they were Mormons. I had guessed that because I knew that Mormons do not drink coffee.

Then, I had the boomerang question: "What could I do or say that would make folks think, 'Ah! He is United Methodist.'" I once saw a sweatshirt with this message: "I am a self-avowed, practicing United Methodist." Apart from a sweatshirt, how would others eavesdrop on me and determine that I am Methodist?

Grace. If it seemed that no matter what the question might be, my answer was "grace"—maybe that is how people could decide that I am Methodist. It is a central theme to Methodist thinking and the core energy for Methodist action.

Grace is God's freely given, undeserved gift. Did you hear of the man who stood at the Pearly Gates, seeking admittance to heaven? St. Peter asked, "Why should you be let into heaven?" "Well," the man replied, "I have attended church all of my life and once went twelve years without missing a Sunday." "That's good," St. Peter answered. "That is worth one point." The man shifted and said, "Not only that, but I have always been kind to children, given large sums of money to help the needy, and gone out of my way to help old folks across the street." "Okay," said the gatekeeper, "that's another point." "Good grief!" the man shouted. "At this rate, I'll only get in by the grace of God!" "Bingo!" said Saint Peter. "Welcome to Heaven."

Have you ever had a teacher say, "If you don't remember anything else I say today, remember. . . ." When I heard that comment, my ears would perk up, in part because I knew what was about to be said was important and in part because I assumed that it would be on the final exam.

If you don't remember anything else about Methodist theology and doctrine, remember this: grace.

Methodists speak of grace in three shapes: prevenient grace, justifying grace, and sanctifying (or perfecting) grace. (More on this in chapter 2, "The Oops.") Methodists are not the only ones who give emphasis to grace. (More on this in chapter 10, "The Others.") Methodists understand that there are some usual ways in which God gives grace. (More on this in chapter 7, "The Means.") Methodists have sometimes lost (misplaced?) the Wesleyan priority on holy living. (More on this in chapter 8, "The Doing.") Methodists know that sometimes a writer must be sneaky to get people to read the rest of the book. (Why do you think I kept saying, "More on this in chapters 2, 10, 7, and 8"?)

What Are You Going to Do About It?

1. Using John Wesley's description of salvation (porch, door, house), how would you depict where you are in your journey right now? Share this self-understanding with someone you trust. Ask if he or she agrees with your self-assessment.
2. Think of four or five of your friends who consider themselves Christian but who come from different church backgrounds (Baptist, Presbyterian, Lutheran, independent, nondenominational, or unaffiliated, for example). How does "salvation" seem to be understood in their traditions? (You could ask, you know.)
3. Imagine that the folks who came up to Jan (in the "Side Trip" above) had come up to you. What would you have said to them? Make a poster that illustrates what you would have said. Could you display the poster at your church?

The Oops

S omewhere along the way I learned this limerick. (If I could remember where I learned it, I'd give credit . . . or blame, as the case might be.)

> God's plan made a hopeful beginning.
> But we spoiled our chances by sinning.
> We trust that the story
> Will end in God's glory
> But at present the other side's winning.

God created the world and got it right (Gen. 1). It was good. Human beings were created in the image of God (Gen. 1:26–27), so we know that human beings were created good. *Original righteousness* is what it is called by people who stay up late at night thinking up what to call these things.

A SIDE TRIP FOR A LITTLE BACKGROUND

Jason stormed out of class. "I have never heard such drivel," he said.

Melika followed Jason and patted him on the shoulder. "What's wrong? I thought that class was great! I learned a lot! What's the problem?"

"What's the problem? Didn't you hear what Mr. Jackson said? He's a heathen, an atheist, and . . .," Jason sputtered, "he's wrong!"

"Whoa! Why do you say all that? I happen to know that Mr. Jackson is a lay speaker at his church. What is all this talk about atheist, heathen, and being wrong?"

"Didn't you hear what he said? He said the earth was created in some kind of Big Bang fourteen billion years ago—or something like that—and then he said that people just sort of evolved from apes or monkeys. That's not what the Bible says, and when it comes to choosing between Old Man Jackson and the Bible, I am going to choose the Bible!"

"Steady, Jason! Steady!" said Melika. "I am a Christian and I think what Mr. Jackson says makes sense. It doesn't make the Bible untrue!"

"How can you say that!" said Jason.

"I don't find the Bible and science in conflict. It's like comparing a ballpoint pen and chocolate cake."

"That is nonsense." Jason was getting riled up with Melika. "You can't compare chocolate cake and ball point pens. They are not the same sort of thing!"

"Precisely," Melika said. "You can chew on a ballpoint pen, but it is not intended for food; you can make a few marks with chocolate cake, but it is not intended for writing."

"So?" Jason was beginning to slow down.

"So, I think the Bible and science are two different kinds of things. You don't expect science to speak of God's relationship with us; you don't expect the Bible to give us scientific information."

Jason paused. "Is this what you are saying—the Bible speaks of who and why; science speaks of when and how?"

Melika laughed. "Now you've given me something to think about!"

And together, the two friends stepped into Ms. Holloman's English class.

Methodists claim that God is Creator. All else is creation. (Check out Col. 1:16.) There is a difference between creator and creature. (Check out Ps. 8:3 and Ps. 95:4–6.) This thought might not seem like a blazingly new insight, but, truth to tell, there is much afoot in the twenty-first century that would challenge this understanding.

Take, for example, astrology: this practice is based on an assumption that the alignment at your birth of the planets and other heavenly bodies influences (predetermines?) what happens in your life.[1] Such a belief flies in the face of the United Methodist teaching that humankind has been given free will (the freedom to make decisions that shape life and even one's relationship with God).[2] Astrology confuses the creator (God) with the creation (stars and planets).[3]

Then there is *New Age*: this loose term has been used to describe everything from finding power through crystals to claiming God is one with the human spirit to saying that God is in the trees (and butterflies and cucumbers and aardvarks). This thinking uses spiritual language but borrows heavily from pantheism, the belief that God is in everything. It is not much of a stretch for New Age philosophy to identify God as tree, God as human spirit, God as rock. Methodists distinguish between God and God's creation.[4]

Humankind is part of the created order. So, humankind was created with the mark of "good" stamped on it. But, oops, something went wrong. The account is told as the story of Adam and Eve, but in a sense it is also my story and your story. Only the names have been changed to protect the guilty! (Adam means "human being"; Eve means "life giver." To worry about whether these were actual people with these actual names can get us sidetracked from the heart of the story.)

The story is told in the book that shows up first in the Bible, Genesis. (The word "genesis" means "beginning." It gets its name not because it is the first book in the Bible, but because it tells about first things: creation, including humankind.) God created Adam and Eve in God's own image (reflection).[5] Being in the image of God suggests at least three things about people: (1) We are created to be in communion with God; (2) we are created to be in relationship with one another; (3) we are to be stewards of God's creation. In these three ways, we are to be reflections (images) of God.

Oops! That original goodness is shattered when Adam and Eve break all three dimensions of being in the image of God: (1) Communion with God? No, they do something God has asked them not to do. Adam hides from God (Gen. 3:6, 10). (2) Relationship with one another? No, in their brokenness from God, they break from one another; suddenly, they are ashamed to be in each other's natural presence and try to hide their nakedness from each other (the fig leaf thing: Gen. 3:7). (3) Stewards of creation? No, in fact Adam and Eve go after the one part of creation that God had said you cared for by leaving alone (Gen. 3:3, 6)!

Finally, there is sin: the condition that separates humankind from God's image. But it gets worse. You and I are painted with the same brush. It is called Original Sin.

A SIDE TRIP FOR A LITTLE BACKGROUND

The protestors all carried large posters, carefully nailed to wooden sticks and waved in the face of everyone who tried to cross their path. They were upset with a television station that had carried a program that showed two women kissing. (This was no peck on the cheek; this was a full, in-your-face, "I want you" kind of kiss.)

One sign read, "This station supports sin." Another one said, "Sin is as close as your nearest TV screen. Turn it off."[6] Kelly wanted to get into the station building because she had the chance to interview Hot Huey for her school paper; Hot Huey was in town for a concert, and to talk to him in person was the opportunity of a lifetime!

Kelly looked at the demonstrators and recognized two girls from her class. They yelled at her, "Hey, Kelly, if you go in there you are supporting sin!" Kelly paused at the door. All kinds of thoughts ran through her head: How does God intend creation to be? Is it wrong for two people in love to kiss one another? Where does my freedom stop and your rights begin? What is sin?

It is called original sin not because it is sin that is unusual or done for the first time. (I'd be hard pressed to think of a sin that has not been committed before! That would make an interesting contest . . . but I stray.) Original sin is called "original" because sin is part of our origins. It is part of the Adam in us! It is part of the human condition.[7]

Some persons try to explain away sin.[8] Popular culture describes human wrongs as mistakes in judgment, psychological pressures, unfortunate backgrounds, social illness. It is not likely that a newspaper will have a headline "Series of Murders Attributed to Sin." Of course, there are indeed circumstances that can be attributed to mistakes in judgment, psychological pressures, unfortunate backgrounds, or social illness. But Methodists have a clear understanding that all persons sin; that is, all persons think and act in ways that are shaped by personal self-service rather than by the will of God: "There is no one who is righteous, not even one" (Rom. 3:10).[9]

A SIDE TRIP FOR A LITTLE BACKGROUND

John Wesley used two terms when he spoke of sin. "Original sin" was the condition put upon all humankind, the result of Adam's fall from original righteousness. Everyone inherits this condition. "Actual sins" were the things persons willingly did that separated them from God and God's intended will.[10]

It is a universal reality. All of us are sinners. All of us are sinful. Some persons in what is sometimes termed "the New Age movement" suggest that by looking within to our inner selves we can find the core goodness that will make us at one with the world and with one another. Not so! Our inner self is also marked by sin. (Some folks use the term "total depravity" to describe this state.)

God does not want things to stay this way. On our own, we human beings cannot do anything about breaking our bondage to sin. (If I get caught touching an open electric wire, I am likely to find the current running through me with, shall we say, shocking results. I cannot break the cycle. But the power can be turned off and I am free.) The power of sin can be broken by the grace of God.

Grace (that word again) is at work in every human being. Methodists call it "prevenient grace." Although it is a little tough to work "prevenient" into a conversation, it is a good Wesleyan word. It means "to come before." This is grace that God gives to every human being, and it is how we are able to come to saving faith in Jesus Christ.

Before we know it, before we claim it, before we can name it, that grace is at work in our lives. (That's one big reason Methodists practice infant baptism, baptizing babies who don't know what is going on; it is the faith community's claim that God is already at work!)

Prevenient grace comes before one believes in Christ. When someone who is not a Christian does something valuable in God's sight—and that happens many, many times—God's prevenient grace makes that possible.[11] Prevenient grace is God's initiative toward humankind; that's how much God wants to heal the breach. This grace—God's free, undeserved gift—makes it possible for people, in their free will, to choose to accept (or not) the gift of faith.

> Before we know it, before we claim it, before we can name it, that grace is at work in our lives.

A SIDE TRIP FOR A LITTLE BACKGROUND

On the computer screen as I type this, there is a place I can click (my right finger on the left mouse button) and justify the margins of this text. Justify it to the left or justify it to the right—when it is justified, it is lined up. Justification occurs when things are lined up right.

God's justifying grace gets us lined up right with God. No wonder that the common language of many in the Christian community describes this grace as being born again! New birth! New life! (The New Testament phrase often translated "born again" can just as well be translated "born from above" [see John 3:3]). This blending of translations reminds us that the new birth is a gift from God.

In justification, God clears the record of our sin. In John Wesley's sermon "The Scripture Way of Salvation," he wrote, "Justification is another word for pardon. It is the forgiveness of all our sins, and (what is necessarily implied therein) our acceptance with God."[12] Methodists believe that whatever is required for us to be pardoned (saved from our sin) has been done by Jesus Christ.

In the Bible Belt, some believers emphasize "getting saved" so one can go to heaven. ("If you were to die tonight, where would you spend eternity?") Methodists are in favor of heaven! Heaven is best marked as eternal fellowship with Jesus Christ. Hell is the absence of that fellowship.

But Methodists understand that being saved is not just a matter of getting into heaven. It is a full gift from God that is even more than heaven! Look up Ephesians 2:8. Here is what John Wesley wrote about that Scripture ("For by grace you have been saved through faith. . . ."):

> The salvation which is here spoken of is not what is frequently understood by that word, the going to heaven, eternal happiness. . . . It is not a blessing which lies on the other side death, or (as we usually speak) in the other world. The very words of the text itself put this beyond all question. 'Ye *are* saved.' It is not something at a distance: it is a present thing, a blessing which, through the free mercy of God, ye are now in possession of. Nay, the words may be rendered, and that with equal propriety, 'Ye *have been* saved.' So that the salvation which is here spoken of might be extended to the entire work of God, from the first dawning of grace in the soul till it is consummated in glory.[13]

What Mr. Wesley was saying—in words that probably flowed more easily in the eighteenth century—was that salvation is more than getting to heaven. Salvation is all that God has done, beginning with planting "salt on our souls so we would thirst for Thee," applying the work of Jesus Christ to us, accepting our repentance and granting us the gift of faith, pardoning our sin, working in us to move toward perfect love, and keeping us in eternal fellowship.

Perfect love? You've got to be kidding! Although a lot of places on the Internet seem to promise that possibility, it is not something that is often a part of the expectation of the Christian community. Methodists think it should be. Perfect love—read about it in chapter 8.

What Are You Going to Do About It?

1. How does sin express itself in your life? Be intentional in identifying ways in which you show a brokenness from God and confess that sin. (Can you find a spiritual partner who will hear your repentance?)
2. Start a list of persons for whom you wish to pray: persons who have not experienced justification, persons who have not shown fruits of sanctification.
3. Choose one person whom you wish to invite to a new relationship with Jesus Christ. How would you go about it?[14]

The People

O kay. Be patient. Stick with me for a moment.

When God created humankind, God decided that people ought to live in relationship with one another (Gen. 2:18).

When God called Moses to go into Egypt and lead the Israelites out of slavery, Moses asked, "Who shall I say sent me to do this?" The answer came: "I am who I am; The God of your ancestors has sent you" (Exod. 3:14–15).

When Moses received the two tablets of the covenant (the Ten Commandments), he knew it was not a gift just for him. It was intended for all the people, and Moses carried it to them (Exod. 31:18; 32:15).

(Keep on hanging; I'll get to the point.)

When many people of the Hebrew nation returned home after an exile in Babylon, Nehemiah, the governor, arranged a covenant (an agreement) between the people and God. It was signed not just by Nehemiah, but by many, many others (Neh. 9:38–10:26).[1]

When Jesus began his public ministry, he gathered around him close associates, the first disciples (Matt. 4:18–22; 10:1–4).

When first-century Christians came to have faith, they did things together (Acts 2:42, 44).

When God wanted to give the gift of the Holy Spirit, God brought that power at Pentecost when the believers were all together (Acts 2:1).

When Saul was converted on the road to Damascus, one of the very first things to happen was God's inspiring Ananias and others to connect Paul with the Christian community (Acts 9:17, 19).

(Still with me?)

When the early church needed to make decisions about the life of faith and how to extend the gospel, they made those decisions together (Acts 15:2; 1 Cor. 8:19).

When the writer of Ephesians wanted to describe Christian life, he used terms like "citizens with the saints" and "members of the household of God" (Eph. 2:19).

When early believers were challenged to set aside sin, they were reminded that it was possible because they were not about it alone (Heb. 12:1).

> Methodists understand the journey of Christian faith to be a corporate experience. It is not a two-seater sports car (just me and Jesus); it is a big bus packed with all kinds of people.

When Christians began to seek healing from their sin, they were advised to confess their sin to one another (Jas. 5:16).

When John had his strange vision, he described heaven not as individuals but as a city, a community, a multitude of believers (Rev. 7:9; 21:2).

Do you see a pattern, a theme, emerging in this quick jaunt through the Bible? God gives the gift of faith ordinarily within *community*. God gives the sustaining means of grace ordinarily within *community*. God gives a setting for living out the faith within *community*.

No wonder that Methodists understand the journey of Christian faith to be a corporate experience. It is not a two-seater sports car (just me and Jesus); it is a big bus packed with all kinds of people. In fact, John Wesley once wrote, "I shall endeavour to show that Christianity is essentially a social religion, and that to turn it into a solitary religion is indeed to destroy it."[2]

A SIDE TRIP FOR A LITTLE BACKGROUND

Methodist life is filled with terms that reflect this understanding that a relationship with Jesus Christ puts one into relationship with other believers. The early Methodist movement was called "The Connexion."[3] Small groups emerged for discipline and growth and searching; they were called "societies" and "bands" and "class meetings." In United Methodism, the word "conference" is used over and over again to describe the meetings at which United Methodists confer with one another. (See chapter 9 for more on this way of doing church life.)

Those words (connexion, society, band, class meeting, and conference) are all words about relationships. My relationship with Jesus Christ is a personal relationship, but it is not private.

Fundamentalism can be one of the more limiting expressions of the Bible Belt. (The five "fundamentals" are the verbal inerrancy of the Scripture, the divinity of Jesus Christ, the virgin birth, a substitutionary theory of the atonement, and the physical resurrection and bodily return of Christ.[4]) What seems interestingly significant about some expressions of fundamentalism is the emphasis on individual decisions without regard to the social nature of the faith event. Methodists are likely to see such individualism as a violation of how God has revealed God's very self to us. (Hold your breath; this gets a little strong.) God has self-revealed God's being as Trinity (see chapter 6 for more). One of the meanings of this doctrine is that God exists as one God in three persons: Father, Son, and Holy Spirit. These three persons exist in one community, the unity of the Godhead.[5] (Okay, you can breathe now.)

If God lives as community and we are created in God's image, we are intended to live in community. God's people model that community. Christians call that community "Church."

A SIDE TRIP FOR A LITTLE BACKGROUND

Carson and Jacqui were longtime friends. Kindergarten. Little League baseball. Cheerleading squad. Honor Society. And church. They grew up together at Mountaintop Church. They had been baptized as infants only three months apart and had made professions of faith the same year at Pentecost. They took turns leading the Wednesday-night youth Bible study.

Faith in Jesus Christ was important to both of them; they often talked about how Christian young adults faced an onslaught of temptations and how hard it could be to hang onto Christian values. They were not "boyfriend/girlfriend," but it was not unusual for one to call the other after a date just to tell how the evening had gone.

So, Jacqui was not surprised when the phone rang late one night and Carson chatted for a while about his evening. As they prepared to hang up, Jacqui said, "Well, see you Sunday at church!"

"Uh, probably," Carson answered.

But he was not at church on Sunday or the next Sunday. Nor was he at Bible study on Wednesday. Jacqui phoned: "Hey, we miss you at church! We need you at Bible study!"

Carson delayed for a moment before he spoke. "Jac, I've been thinking. I don't think I'll be at church for a while, if at all." His words began to flood out: "It's not that I don't like you and the others; it's just that I have decided that I need to spend more time with Jesus. The most important thing to me is how I get along with Jesus. I think I can do that best if I go it alone. Now, I am still a Christian and I'm trying hard to be a better Christian, but I think all that church stuff is a distraction. It gets in the way. I don't want you to take this the wrong way, but I'm not sure that the Church is needed."

Jacqui swallowed hard.

The Confession of Faith of the Evangelical United Brethren Church (remember: one of the denominations that formed the United Methodist Church) says this about the Church:

We believe the Christian Church is the community of all true believers under the Lordship of Christ. We believe it is one, holy, apostolic, and catholic. It is the redemptive fellowship in which the

Word of God is preached by (persons) divinely called, and the sacraments are duly administered according to Christ's own appointment. Under the discipline of the Holy Spirit the Church exists for the maintenance of worship, the edification of believers and the redemption of the world.[6]

Let's walk through that statement of belief:

Community: The Christian Church is made up of relationships held in common. It is the one community, not one of many different communities.[7]

All true believers: The presence of authentic faith is essential for the existence of the Church. The boundaries are not those of class, race, ethnic background, nationality, or gender.[8]

Lordship of Christ: The life and mission of the Church is an expression of the rule and reign of Jesus Christ. Decisions of the Church are to be measured by Jesus Christ.[9]

One: The unity of the Church is in Jesus Christ. Although human frailty has led to the fragmentation of the Church, it is God's will that we all be one.[10]

Holy: The Church is called to be different, what the King James Version of the Bible called "a peculiar people." The difference is a personal and a social holiness (standards set apart from the world).[11]

Apostolic: The Church stands in solidarity with the witness of the apostles. The teaching of the Church is to be the teaching of the apostles.[12]

Catholic: Because of the wide presence of the Roman Catholic Church, some persons believe the term "catholic" applies only to that group of Christians. Not so! The word "catholic" simply means universal, embracing an invitation to all people and expressing the fullness of faithful teaching.[13]

Redemptive fellowship: The Church is the community ordinarily used by God to present the claim of the Gospel and ordinarily used by God to move people into faith and holy living.[14]

Word of God: This term (sometimes applied to Jesus Christ) means what God has to say. In Jesus, the Word came and lived among us.[15]

Preached by (persons) divinely called: The Church is the community that sets apart those who are to preach the Word. Such proclamation is one of the signs of the existence of the Church.[16]

Sacraments duly administered: The Lord's Supper and holy baptism are these gifts of God's grace given through the Church (more on this in chapter 6 and chapter 7).[17]

Christ's own appointment: One of the characteristics of a sacrament is that it is commanded by Christ. Jesus Christ is uniquely present in the sacraments.[18]

Discipline of the Holy Spirit: "Discipline" and "disciple" have the same roots; God's Spirit directs, shapes, and corrects the Church in the search for faithful discipleship.[19]

Maintenance of worship: The very reason for the Church's existence is the worship of God. Worship is not about me (how I feel); it is about God.[20]

Edification of believers: "Edification?" Think edifice: building. The Church helps to build up (strengthen, grow, nurture) those who trust Christ.[21]

Redemption of the world: The Church is a model of what God intends for all creation, everything and everyone reconciled with God.[22]

A SIDE TRIP FOR A LITTLE BACKGROUND

Robert Carl slipped into the back row of the fellowship hall, just in time to hear the "Amen" that closed the opening prayer for the meeting of the church council of the Kudzu Memorial United Methodist Church. Even as he sat down, he could sense the tension in the room. It had all the feeling of a showdown at O.K. Corral. Where was Wyatt Earp when you needed him?

At first the gathering unfolded in typical ways: minutes approved, appreciation expressed to the men for sponsoring a Lay Witness Mission, plans described for the fall youth retreat, and decisions made about who should mow the church lawn.

Then came the treasurer's report. It was obvious that this was why attendance was so high for this council meeting. Members stirred and some sat on the edge of the hard folding chairs. Robert leaned forward so he could hear everything.

Treasurer Kenneth Charles said, "I sent that money to missions because I cannot stand to hear about hungry children. It was, as you know, an emergency. What is this church about if it is not about helping hungry people? After all, we said our goal was to use 50 percent of our money for others."

"Now, we all want to help people," spoke up Jane Gregson. "The problem is that no one told you to spend that money. You just did it on your own!"

"Well, what else was he to do?" interrupted Julio Gonzalez. "Wait until those children starved?"

"I think we do enough of things like that," Harry McIntire said, jumping into the fray. "It is about time we thought about keeping the home fires burning."

"Well, I just tell it as I see it," broke in a tall woman Robert did not know. "Our treasurer has spent money that we did not authorize. Where I come from, that is stealing!"

"How dare you call me a thief!" shouted Kenneth Charles. "I was just trying to help! If you think you can do a better job, why don't you try to be treasurer for a while!"

No one noticed when Robert Carl slipped out of his seat at the back. He went home and with anger in his eye said to his mother, "Church is not supposed to be like that. I think I'd be better off without church."

Church as we experience it at the corner of Main Street and Goshen Highway might not match up very well with the high-flung biblical descriptions of Church. The Church on earth is often a pale reflection of the image to which God calls God's people. Even when we fall short of that destiny, Methodists maintain that God's intent and ultimate will is a "building from God, a house not made with hands."[23] Maybe it is like this: when Jesus walked on earth, we got a glimpse of God's reign, what it would be like when God's rule is fully realized. There still was evil; there still was illness; there still was brokenness. But in Jesus Christ we got a glimpse of God's intent. So now the Church, the body of Christ today, gives us a glimpse of what is yet an invisible Church. In the mystery of God, the Word became flesh and lived among us as a human being, a perfect human one; in the mystery of God, the Church now lives in the world as human beings, imperfect, but the channel of God's perfect grace.

"But we have this treasure in clay jars, so that it may be made clear that this extraordinary power belongs to God and does not come from us."[24] God ordinarily has chosen to give that extraordinary power through community. That's why Methodists stick with the Church.

What Are You Going to Do About It?

1. Get in touch with those responsible for nominating persons for places of service within your local church. (For United Methodists, the pastor chairs the committee on lay leadership.) Let them know of your willingness to serve, and identify others whom you recommend for service.
2. Find out all you can about the history of your local church. Can you help the committee on records and history prepare a display?
3. Arrange for a study of Article 13 ("Of the Church") in the Articles of Religion shared by the United Methodist Church, the African Methodist Episcopal Church, the African Methodist Episcopal Zion Church, and the Christian Methodist Episcopal Church.

The Book

All right. I'll admit it. You have probably already heard this one. It is number thirty-seven in the list of standard jokes told by most preachers:

A brother and sister look over into the corner of their living room and see elderly Granny hard at work reading the Bible. "What is she doing?" asked the boy. His sister replied, "Oh, I think she is cramming for her finals."

And this one?

W. C. Fields was a curmudgeon.[1] Once, when he was caught reading the Bible, a skeptical friend asked him what he was doing. Fields is reputed to have replied, "Ah! I've spent a lot of time searching through the Bible for loopholes."

One more:

Ambrose Bierce, almost a hundred years ago, wrote in *The Devil's Dictionary*, "Christian, noun: one who believes that the New Testament is a divinely inspired book admirably suited to the spiritual needs of his neighbor."[2]

Now we come to John Wesley. In a preface to a collection of his sermons, he wrote, "I want to know one thing, the way to heaven—how to land safe on that happy shore. God himself has condescended to teach the way: for this very end he came from heaven.[3] He hath written it down in a book. O give me that book! At any price give me the Book of God! I have it. Here is knowledge enough for me. Let me be *homo unius libri* (a man of one book)."[4]

Methodists believe that the primary authority for the Christian journey, for Christian thought, and for Christian action is Holy Scripture. (Methodists accept as Holy Scripture the sixty-six books of the Bible generally acknowledged by Protestants.)[5] The Scripture contains everything one needs to know in order to be saved; for Methodists, that is why God has revealed God's purposes in the Bible.[6] (Remember that for Methodists, salvation includes repentance, justification, sanctification, and glorification.)

Students of the Bible today often point to the various points of view that are represented in the Bible. (For example, Matthew was written primarily to a Jewish readership; Luke might have been aimed at a more non-Jewish audience.) Careful readers of the Bible will discover that sometimes the text is written as poetry (Psalms), sometimes as correspondence (1 Corinthians), sometimes as legal requirements (Leviticus), sometimes as story (Ruth), sometimes as warning (Obadiah), sometimes as imagery (Revelation), sometimes as history (1 Samuel), sometimes as legend (Genesis), sometimes as gospel (John).

Methodists are willing to be rigorous in biblical scholarship; there is no reason to fear Truth; it comes from God. Therefore, even though there are many angles and numerous styles, there is a unity in the biblical message. The God of the Old Testament is the God of the New Testament.[7] The one revelation is of a God who created, loves, and seeks to save humankind and the rest of the created order.

A statement on "Our Theological Task" includes for United Methodists the sense in which there is a balance between the range within the Bible and the oneness of the witness: "Scripture witnesses to a variety of diverse traditions, some of which reflect tensions in interpretation within the early Judeo-Christian heritage. However, these traditions are woven together in the Bible in a manner that expresses the fundamental unity of God's revelation as received and experienced by people in the diversity of their own lives."[8]

A SIDE TRIP FOR A LITTLE BACKGROUND

What started as a pleasant dorm Bible study quickly got kind of rough. After an opening prayer ("Oh, Lord, meet us in Your

Word . . ."), Jon began the discussion by saying, "I'm glad we can explore God's Word together. It is the one thing that we know is true."

Kevin blurted out, "I don't know that it is all true! What about that bit about a big fish swallowing Jonah and then upchucking him so he could keep on preaching?"

Jon tried to stay calm. "Now, we all know that if it is in the Bible, then it happened." He added for emphasis, "Just as the Bible says."

Kevin lashed back, "Maybe that is a story to make a point and not a historic fact!"

Jon began to lose what cool he had. "Are you saying that the Bible is not entirely true?"

"Let me try this out on you," responded Kevin. "Do you think Jesus went around saying 'Baaaa'?"

"Of course not."

"But the Bible calls Him the Lamb of God. Don't lambs go 'baaa'?"

"But that's different. It's a figure of speech."

"And do you think that it is the only figure of speech in the Bible?"

"God says it. I believe it. That does it."

By now Perry and Marsh joined the fray.

"That kind of religious narrow-mindedness makes things too simple. Life is too complex for such easy yes/no, black/white, right/wrong answers!"

"I agree! I'm tired of you folks who think that you don't have to think!"

Jon was on the defensive: "You are distorting the Bible. It says what it says. If God wanted it to say something else, it would say something else!"

Kevin jumped back in: "You are worshiping those pages and not the God of the Book!"

A quiet came over the room.

Some Christians think the Bible is inerrant, that is, without any error of fact, be it of science or geography or history. Some Christians think the Bible is infallible, that is, without any human filters in its original texts. Methodists have not been immune from these views. However, a literal view of the Bible does not take into account differences in the way various biblical writers tell the story of what God has been doing. (Did God create all things in seven days? How could creation have occurred in what we know as seven twenty-four hour days when Genesis 1:14 says that it was not until the fourth "day" that there was any division between day and night?)

A literal view of the Bible does not take into account how some of the texts address issues that were specific to one time and place and not necessarily to all times and places. (Does it seem appropriate for Christians to implement Deuteronomy 21:18–21 which calls for stoning to death a disobedient son?)

A literal view of the Bible does not take into account the way Jesus reflected on Scripture. For example, Jesus interpreted Scripture as having meaning far beyond the exact dictionary meaning of the words of the text. In Matthew 5:21, Jesus quotes Exodus 20:13—"You shall not murder"—but says the prohibition means far more than just literally killing people. Jesus says the prohibition includes getting angry with those in the community (Matt. 5:22).

> John Wesley believed in the plain meaning of the biblical text but understood that the plain meaning was not always the literal meaning. He believed that the Bible was twice inspired: once when written and again when read.

A literal view does not take into account the use of images and figures of speech in the Scriptures. Look at Psalm 64:7: does God really shoot people with a bow and arrow? Look at Isaiah 37:29: does the Lord really grab people with a physical hook? Look at Matthew 6:6: does God really only listen to prayers that are prayed behind closed doors?

John Wesley introduced his collection of biblical sermons by writing "I desire plain truth for plain people."[9] Wesley believed in the plain meaning of the biblical text but understood that plain meaning was not always the literal meaning. He believed that the Bible was twice inspired: once when written and again when read.

In some ways, strains and divisions within the United Methodist Church today come from disagreement about which of these two points to emphasize: inspired when written or inspired when read. In one case, the reader is concerned only with the precise wording of the original manuscript, with little regard to its cultural context or historical setting. In the other case, the reader is concerned with bringing to bear on the biblical text all of the influences of modern sociology, psychology, geography, and economics with little regard for the meaning offered in the ancient text. Methodists in the Wesleyan tradition balance these two extremes, aware that the same Holy Spirit who inspired the Scriptures is alive and well to bring the written Word alive for the twenty-first century. We take seriously both the original inspiration and today's contemporary inspiration.

So, how did John Wesley sort through the Scriptures when there seemed to be conflicts, vagueness, uncertainty? In the preface to his standard sermons (1746), he spelled out how he studied the Bible:

Here then I am, far from the busy ways of men. I sit down alone: only God is here. In his presence I open, I read his Book; for this end, to find the way to heaven. Is there a doubt concerning the meaning of what I read? Does anything appear dark or intricate? I lift up my heart to the Father of lights: "Lord, is it not thy Word, 'If any man lack wisdom, let him ask of God'? Thou 'givest liberally and upbraidest not.' Thou hast said, 'If any be willing to do thy will, he shall know.' I am willing to do, let me know, thy will." I then search after and consider parallel passages of Scripture, "comparing spiritual things with spiritual." I meditate thereon, with all the attention and earnestness of which my mind is capable. If any doubt still remains, I consult those who are experienced in the things of God, and then the writing whereby, being dead, they yet speak. And what I thus learn, that I teach.[10]

Methodists who seek to study the Bible in this Wesleyan pattern will (1) set aside a time and place where such reading can occur without interruption; (2) accept the presence of God's Holy Spirit; (3) read with an openness to new places God might lead; (4) pursue difficult passages by praying, comparing other biblical texts, meditating on possible meanings, connecting with others in the community of believers, and drawing on the understandings of the ancient tradition.

In this way, the Bible itself becomes the balancing, clarifying, even correcting tool for understanding the Scripture. God's gifts in the written Word are so rich that they can continue to give light and life as one digs again and again into the same Scriptures. God's inspired Word is as fresh as the love God brings anew each day.[11]

A SIDE TRIP FOR A LITTLE BACKGROUND

The youth Sunday School class at Murkey Memorial UM/AME/AMEZ/CME Church was restless. Class members could hear some of the other classes begin to roam the halls on their way to the worship service. Most of the boys and girls were ready to go, but Mrs. Womble was determined to teach right up to the last moment.

Fred Womble shifted in his chair as his aunt, the teacher, said, "So, if the Bible is not always to be taken literally, just how is it to be taken?"

(Interest picked up a bit. Why hadn't she started the class time with that question?)

"I just read a book," she continued (*Note: It was this very book, dear reader, which you hold in your hand*), "that told of several verses that we should not take literally. Just how are we to take them?"

"Next Sunday, maybe," whispered one class member.

"For example," Mrs. Womble went on, "if Genesis 1 is not a scientific account of how things began, what is God trying to tell us in those verses?"

There was silence. The squirming stopped.

"The point of those verses is the truth that God is responsible for all of the creation. The rest of the story is the way that truth is packaged. Don't confuse the wrappings with the gift."

"My little sister would rather play with the paper her birthday paper is wrapped in than play with the present," said Sherica Jones.

"Exactly! And some folks read the Bible that way, more interested in the way the truth is wrapped than they are in the truth itself." Mrs. Womble had the class's interest now. "In that book I read, it said that sometimes the Bible is aimed at a particular issue in another time, like Deuteronomy 21:18–21, which calls for stoning disobedient sons."

There were nervous giggles in the room.

"What is the truth in those verses?"

James Andrews ventured an answer: "Obeying parents is important. Is that it?"

"I'm sure that is part of the truth. But notice that those verses say that the parents ought to talk with the community about the problem. Do you suppose the Bible is teaching us that we are responsible for one another, responsible for our neighbor?"

"That surely beats getting killed with a stone dropped on me!" said James.

"And this book I read—oh, it is a wonderful book!—says that sometimes Jesus spelled out a truth that was bigger than the literal words of a verse. For example, Exodus 20:13, from the Ten Commandments, says, 'You shall not murder,' or as some old translations say, 'Thou shalt not kill.' When Jesus referred to that verse he said the bigger truth was more than just killing; the truth of the verse is that even getting bent out of shape with someone can be wrong!"

"Did Jesus say 'get bent out of shape'?" asked Fred.

"Not exactly, but I think that is what he meant. Check it out. It is in Matthew 5:22."

By now the class was ignoring the noises from the hallway and was listening closely to Mrs. Womble.

"Let me give you one to work on," she said. "Try Psalm 64:7."

The youth found Psalms in the time-honored way: they held up their Bibles and opened them in the middle. It did not take long to find number 64.

Fred read it aloud, "But God will shoot his arrow at them." He paused. "Who is 'them'?"

"Read a few verses ahead," offered Sherica. "'Them' is folks who try to be sneaky thinking God won't notice them."

"Does God use a bow and arrow?" asked Fred.

"No!" said Sherica. "That verse means you can't fool God! You can't sneak around and do bad things and think that God does not see you!"

"That makes more sense than the literal meaning!"

"Hey!" said Mrs. Womble, "I think I hear the praise choir starting the service. We had better get over there!"

Some people in the Bible Belt say they want their Bible unvarnished. "I'll take my Bible straight." One problem with that approach is that even my reading of the Bible goes through the filters of my sinfulness. No wonder I can prove pretty much what I want to by quoting Bible verses picked out to confirm my point! Second Peter 3:16 addresses the same point: speaking of the letters of Paul, the writer says, "There are some things in them hard to understand, which the ignorant and unstable twist to their own destruction, as they do the other scriptures."

The earliest Methodists in this country passed on to us the central importance of remaining immersed in the Scriptures. Francis Asbury, one of the first two bishops of Methodism in America, wrote on August 26, 1779:

> The Bible provides not so much a detailed map for that journey as it does a compass: directions that move us closer to God and to neighbor.

This morning, I ended the reading my Bible through, in about four months. It is hard work for me to find time for this; but all I read and write, I owe to early rising. If I were not to rise always by five, and sometimes at four o'clock, I should have no time only to eat my breakfast, pray in the family, and get ready for my journey—as I must travel every day.[12]

We must travel too. Life is a journey for each of us. The Bible provides not so much a detailed map for that journey as it does a compass: directions that move us closer to God and to neighbor.

What Are You Going to Do About It?

1. Start a daily discipline of reading the Bible. Your pastor or director of Christian education can suggest tools for this practice.
2. Consider being a part of a Bible study group. Find out about Disciple Bible Study (studies for youth and for adults) by contacting Cokesbury at 1-800-672-1789.
3. Choose one of the gospel accounts (Matthew, Mark, Luke, or John) and read it straight through in one sitting.

The Guide

I t's funny the way traditions get started. Some say that the custom of standing when choirs sing the "Hallelujah Chorus" began because the king stood up at one of the early performances, so everyone else stood up in respect. The United States has its own parallel: the seventh-inning stretch at a baseball game first happened when President Taft was attending a game; he got up to leave in the seventh inning; the crowd stood to honor the President.[1] Folks have been standing during the seventh inning ever since.

So it is with the quadrilateral. Nice word: quadrilateral. (It is a little hard to work into non-Methodist conversations.) It means "four sides." No one meant to create a quadrilateral. It just happened, sort of like the seventh-inning stretch.

For a little more than a quarter of a century, Methodists have referred to the quadrilateral as the "Wesley quadrilateral," although Mr. Wesley would not have known the term any more than he would have known about "adverse camber."[2] This five-syllable mouthful has been part of United Methodist vocabulary at least since 1972 when *The Book of Discipline* adopted that year made "the assertion that contemporary doctrinal reflection and construction in The United Methodist Church should be guided by four *interdependent* sources or guidelines: Scripture, tradition, experience, and reason."[3] (Four sides, get it?) In fact, although "quadrilateral" is used frequently in United Methodist circles, it is not part of official church language.[4] It has just become the way United Methodists talk.

And why not? The four sides (Scripture, tradition, experience, reason) are the guides, the filters, the boundaries, the sources for Methodist theological thought. In contrast, some modern traditions insist that reason be the prime deciding factor for religious thought. Other persons want a literal reading of biblical text to be normative. Some Christian denominations draw most heavily on tradition in making decisions. Often, in contemporary church life, religious meaning is measured primarily by what persons feel and experience.[5] The quadrilateral is one way that persons in the Wesleyan tradition seek to blend and balance all four of these sources: Scripture, tradition, experience, reason.

> The quadrilateral is one way that persons in the Wesleyan tradition seek to blend and balance all four of these sources: Scripture, tradition, experience, reason.

John Wesley frequently brought together "knowledge" and "feeling" as he preached the fullness of salvation. "You see, you know, you feel, God is all in all."[6]

Charles Wesley weaved both knowing and feeling, both mind and heart, into his hymns of Christian assurance (the emphasis is mine):

How can we sinners *know* our sins on earth forgiven?
How can my gracious Savior *show* my name inscribed in heaven?

What we have *felt* and *seen*, with confidence we tell,
And publish to the ends of earth the signs infallible.
We who in Christ believe that he for us hath died,
We all his unknown peace receive and *feel* his blood applied.

We by his Spirit *prove* and *know* the things of God,
The things which freely of his love he hath on us bestowed.

The meek and lowly heart that in our Savior was,
To us that Spirit doth impart and signs us with his cross.

Our nature's turned, our *minds* transformed in all its powers,
And both the witnesses are joined, the Spirit of God with ours.[7]

A SIDE TRIP FOR A LITTLE BACKGROUND

Charles Wesley was John's younger brother. Both of them studied at Christ Church of Oxford University. (In spite of the name, "Christ Church" is a college, not a congregation.) When Charles was at the university, John thought his brother was not spending enough time in study and other scholarly pursuits. Charles enjoyed the exciting life of parties and dancing and music and sports at Oxford. When John cautioned him (older brothers sometimes do that, you know), Charles replied, "Would you have me become a saint all at once?"

Truth to tell, Charles was not really such a wild sort. He and some friends began meeting to try to strengthen their lives in the Christian faith: Bible study, prayer, helping the poor, visiting the prisons, spiritual accountability. When John (now ordained a priest in the Church of England) returned to Oxford as a fellow (a tutor), Charles asked him to assist this group of friends. Of course, anyone who looked very religious stood out at Oxford in those days, so this group got teased and mocked. Some called them "Bible Moths." Others labeled them the "Godly Club." For some, this was the "Holy Club." The group was so methodical in its approach to Christian living that often other students called them "Methodists." That name stuck.[8]

Charles had a splendid ministry of preaching and singing. He wrote thousands of hymns, many of which are standards in much of Christendom: "Hark! The Herald Angels Sing"; "Love Divine, All Loves Excelling"; "Oh, For a Thousand Tongues to Sing"; "Christ the Lord Is Risen Today"; "Jesus, Lover of My Soul"; and "Ah, the Lovely Appearance of Death." (Okay! So some of the thousands of hymns are not winners; forget "Lovely Appearance"; it was not one of his better efforts.)

Hymns have been so important in Methodist practice that one might even consider the table of contents of the *United Methodist Hymnal* an outline of Wesleyan theology.

Thank you, Charles!

Of the four sides (or sources or guides) included in the quadrilateral, without question Scripture is the base. Although the biblical text "talks" with reason, tradition, and experience, "United Methodists share with other Christians the conviction that Scripture is the primary source and criterion for Christian doctrine."[9] No matter what we learn from experience, appreciate in tradition, and gain from reason, if faith and practice are not faithful to the Scripture, they are faulty.

So, using the quadrilateral is not a matter of seeing which source is most persuasive; the quadrilateral is using reason, experience, and tradition to appropriate the honest and full message of the Bible. Reason, experience, and tradition are subservient to Scripture.

Methodists have come to understand that the "honest and full message" of the Bible is most likely to be revealed to those who draw on reason, tradition, and experience. Such an approach to Bible study tends to protect Methodists from "bibliolatry" (which is a kind of worship of the Bible instead of the God of the Bible). The Bible is the final authority, and persons in the Wesleyan pattern will use reason, tradition, and experience as the lenses through which to look at the Scripture. (Think of it like this: I wear glasses and unless I have them on, even though I want very much to see the words on my computer screen, the text blurs. Even though God has revealed plain truth in the Bible, we sometimes need the help of experience, tradition, and reason to bring the meaning of the text into focus.)

> Some called them "Bible Moths." Others labeled them the "Godly Club." For some, this was the "Holy Club." The group was so methodical in its approach to Christian living that often other students called them "Methodists." That name stuck.

What about reason? It is a way we order (organize) information and insights. It is a way we test idea one with idea two to see if the two ideas are consistent. Sometimes it is just common sense. Sometimes it is careful, critical thought. When the grace of God is allowed to work in a life, reason can become a tool of that grace.

Reason describes how God is at work in what God has created. Reason does not operate in a vacuum. Reason does not produce independent information; it processes data from other sources.[10] In a letter sent to an old friend, John Wesley wrote: "'[Some say] you are for reason; I am for faith.' I am for both: for faith to perfect my reason, that, by the Spirit of God not putting out the eyes of my understanding but enlightening them more and more. I may 'be ready to give a clear', scriptural 'answer to every man that asketh me a reason of the hope that is in me.'"[11]

Methodists do not shy away from reason and learning. There is an expectation that clergy will be educated.[12] United Methodists in the United States have thirteen schools of theology, one medical college, ninety-two four-year colleges and universities, eight two-year colleges, and nine preparatory schools.[13] Keep in mind that this list does not include the many academic institutions of other denominations in the Methodist family and does not represent educational settings outside of the United States.

Reason needs the power of grace to overcome its "bent to sinning." God gives such grace; and reason becomes an instrument for clarity in faith, consistency in witness, and freshness in understanding.

What about tradition? John Wesley gave the greatest value to the teaching and practice of the ancient Church (up through the fourth century) and to the Church of England of his own time (1700s). Wesley read widely and deeply in the writings of the earliest Christian thinkers.[14]

In a sense, Methodists have Jewish roots deeper than Christian roots. (Our predecessors in faith were Jewish longer than they were Christian.) And, in a sense, Methodists have longer Roman Catholic roots than Protestant roots. (We were Roman Catholic longer than we have been Protestant.) And in a sense, Methodists have fuller Protestant roots than they do Church of England roots. (We were Protestant before there was Church of England.) When Christian belief moved out of the Jewish tradition, it did not abandon all the power of Jewish heritage. When the Protestant Reformation led some of the Church apart from Roman Catholicism, it did not mean that there was no longer any meaning in the faithful teachings of Roman Catholic scholars. And when the Church of England became one expression of the Protestant Reformation, it did not mean that all other Protestant thought was no longer relevant. When Methodism began to breathe separately from the Church of England, it did not mean that all was to be forgotten about the Anglican faith.

Tradition is not without sin and mistake. Scripture is still the standard, but tradition represents how God has moved among cultures and peoples to move the gospel from one generation to the next. The prophet Isaiah grasped that reality when he wrote, "Go now, write it before them on a tablet, and inscribe it in a book, so that it may be for the time to come as a witness forever."[15]

The writer of Deuteronomy named tradition in this manner: "When your children ask you in time to come, 'What is the meaning of the decrees and the statutes and the ordinances that the Lord your God has commanded you?' then you shall say to your children, 'We were Pharaoh's slaves in Egypt, but the Lord brought us out of Egypt with a mighty hand.'"[16] The writer was penning this six hundred years after the exodus, six hundred years after the Hebrews had escaped from Egypt, but the writer still used the word "we." *We* were Pharaoh's slaves . . . the Lord brought *us* out with a mighty hand. Even though it was six centuries later, the writer of Deuteronomy knew that indeed this was more than just a story about "back then"; it is also *our* story! He wrote it as if he had been there!

That is the power of tradition. It is not a matter of trying to remember how we have always done it.[17] That would be traditionalism, getting stuck in the past. Listening to tradition is having a conversation with those who first climbed the mountain, asking them where the rocks might be and what the view is like. There is an arrogance in not talking with the ancients. Would we dare to say that God was not alive and well in those days?

And what about experience?

A SIDE TRIP FOR A LITTLE BACKGROUND

Legend has it (that means I can't remember where I heard this story) that a native tribe in South America had an unusual way of speaking. The grammar for this tribal language called for one of three phrases to be used at the end of any sentence. One phrase meant "This is a rumor." Another meant "I have this on good authority." The third phrase meant "I have seen it for myself."

Today, such a way of talking could create some interesting moments. Suppose you are in a shopping mall trying to spot a new swimsuit for the upcoming beach season. The clerk looks at you modeling the new outfit and says, "Oh, yes, that swimsuit is definitely you. This is a rumor." Or an irate parent yells at his son,

"When I was your age I never did anything like that! This is a rumor." Hmmm. Interesting.

But it could be quite telling in faith conversations. "God loves me. This is a rumor." Or, "The Bible says God loves me. At least, I have it on good authority." Or, perhaps, "God loves me. I have seen it for myself."

Experience is about seeing it for ourselves. (Even though this is a personal journey, it is hardly without the gift of the community: witness, tradition, love.) Often in church thought, persons have spoken of the value of reason and tradition as ways of confirming the Scriptures. The added dimension brought by John Wesley's thought (and preserved in Methodism) was that God's grace could be seen for real in the lives of people: experience. One way that Wesley expressed that was by keeping meticulous diaries and journals of his own experience in the journey of grace. (He kept a diary for sixty-five years; he wrote in his journals for fifty-five years.)[18] Another way that early Methodists celebrated the experience of God among "ordinary people" was the extensive use of biographies in magazines and books. The story of the Scripture's truth could be told with living evidence: people's lives!

Even though this is a personal journey, it is hardly without the gift of the community: witness, tradition, love.

There is a danger in an emphasis on experience. Some persons become so thrilled by what God has done in their lives that they expect others to have exactly the same experience of God. (Old-time Bible Belt revivals often expected all persons to answer an altar call as the chief evidence that God was at work in their lives. Those faithful who could not name the hour and place of this experience would be considered second-rate Christians.) By way of contrast, the statement "Our Theological Task" in the United Methodist *Book of Discipline* calls experience "richly varied."[19] Standing alone, experience is a poor conductor of the electricity of faith. If experience is the only standard for truth, then truth becomes relative, sort of "what do I feel like today." It is not enough just to say, "It must be God because it makes me feel good." But experience—my experience, your experience, our experience—is a vital voice in the conversation with Scripture, tradition, and reason.

What Are You Going to Do About It?

1. Put down this book right now and write an entry for your new journal. Once I decided that I did not have to be profound and full of brilliant insight each day, I found it easier to keep the habit going. Just start with a note about what you have done today. Sometime in the future, you will find yourself noting something of significant meaning in your life. (My family understands that they are not to read my journal until after I am dead.)
2. Pick up this book and start reading again.
3. Tell all your friends how wonderful this book is and encourage them to buy dozens of copies.
4. Read the biography or autobiography of some of the saints of the faith, both those well known and those who are little known.[20]
5. No, I mean it. Put this book down and start your journal!

The Start

Scene One: The congregation chuckles as an embarrassed mother and father bring their screaming baby to the pastor. Quiet decorum is no match for the new set of lungs. Finally, after leading the way through the stories of God's saving work, assurance of church support, and promises of Christian intent, the pastor dips his hand into a small bowl of water and says, "Louise Antoinette, I baptize you in the name of the Father, and of the Son, and of the Holy Spirit. Amen." Then, the pastor turns to the congregation, lifts up the child and says, "Here, my brothers and sisters, is the world's newest Christian."

Scene Two: It had sounded like a good plan: Easter Sunday morning at Lake Hopatcong. Now on the chilly late March morning, everyone remembered that Easter came early this year! Breeze blew in off the lake and the gathered congregation shivered, but Pastor Diane Greenwood knew she would proceed as planned. "Easter," she said, "is not about spring flowers and warm weather. It is about new life in Jesus Christ." Then, she stepped out into the lake with Julio and Marcella Gomez. One after the other, she lowered them three times under the water, saying, "I baptize you in the name of the Father, and of the Son, and of the Holy Spirit. Amen."

Scene Three: Jeffrey Johnson knelt and bowed his head. This was the moment toward which the recent year of his sixteen-year-old life had pointed. The Reverend Mr. Merritt completed the prayer of thanksgiving and then poured a large flow of water over Jeff's head. The water splashed loudly into a brass basin. With water trickling past his ears, running down his neck, and thoroughly wetting his hair, Jeff heard, "Jeffrey Richard, I baptize you in the name of the Father, and of the Son, and of the Holy Spirit. Amen." Some of the moisture in the basin now came from Jeff's tears of joy.

Scene Four: For years, the Happy Helpers Sunday School class had dreamed of going together on a trip to the Holy Lands. After fund-raisers and many special offerings and personal savings, twelve members of the class stood on the banks of the Jordan River. "Maybe our Lord Jesus was baptized here or in a place very much like this," their guide said. Class president Mildred Shuler turned to Pastor Graham. "It would mean so much to me, and probably to all of us, if you could baptize us again here in the Jordan River! I would remember it forever!" The pastor rubbed his hand under his chin, and said, "Let me tell you why I could not baptize you a second time, here or anywhere else."

Any of these four scenes could have occurred among Methodist people. Baptism includes infants, teens, and adults. Baptism can be by sprinkling a little water, pouring a lot of water, or even immersing the candidate totally in water. Baptism is done in the name of the Father, the Son, and the Holy Spirit. And baptism is done only once.

Baptism is about the activity of God. (It is done *in the name of* God: Father, Son, Holy Spirit.) Baptism is a statement and an enactment and the fulfillment of God's promise of grace. God does not go back on God's promises; that is why Methodists do not baptize persons more than once. To baptize someone a second time is to say that God did not keep God's promise of grace. Of course, we human beings slip and slide in our efforts to keep our end of the agreement with God, but God is steadfast and faithful.

> God does not go back on God's promises; that is why Methodists do not baptize persons more than once.

Baptism is having "property of God" stamped on one's life, and that claim by God cannot be erased. It is the sacrament of Christian initiation offered both to those who come to faith and repent (Acts 2:38; 8:13; 9:18; 22:16) and to those who are born into the household of faith (Acts 16:15; 16:33; Matt. 19:13–15).

Many traditions within the Bible Belt practice only "believer's baptism." (This means that persons are baptized only when they can make a meaningful confession of Christian faith.) Methodists, on the other hand, have seen infant baptism as normative, although in today's culture many persons are adults before they have their first personal relationship with the community of faith. The baptism of babies makes sense only in the context of a covenant community that can nurture and bring the child to a profession of faith. Methodists, therefore, are giving renewed consideration to the practice of baptizing persons who are new to the faith community as adults, because many in today's culture do not grow up within the family of faith.[1]

Can a person be saved without being baptized? Yes. But the ordinary means by which God incorporates persons into the faith is baptism. Baptism itself is "a means of justification and regeneration, that is, that those who have been baptized have been justified and born again."[2]

A SIDE TRIP FOR A LITTLE BACKGROUND

Language about "being born again" and "new birth" and "regeneration" has been used in various Christian heritages. (I once completed a biographical form for a group to whom I was to speak; it asked, "Have you been born again? If so, when?" My answer was "Yes, I have been born again. When? A.D. 29. That's when Jesus died on the cross and rose from the dead.")

The New Testament Greek word translated "born again" (as in John 3:3) is *anothen*. The word can mean "again" or "from above" or "from the top" or "from the first." What was Jesus saying?

Methodists have understood that Jesus was inviting followers to a new birth from above. (It is *both* "born again" and "born from above"!) Being born again from above is the beginning of the journey toward holiness. (Remember chapter 1?) If you want some big words to use (perhaps to impress a few friends), you could say that regeneration is about justification as the start of a journey of sanctification.

Methodists often come to a position of balance between strongly opposed views. Rather than an "either/or" theology, Methodists often move toward a "both/and" theology. This approach to critical thought is the full harvest of a beginning point of the energy of God's grace coupled with an awareness of human free will. (In other words, even though God *could* make us love God, God chooses not *to make us* love God. God initiates the relationship and invites us to respond. This understanding balances the power of God and the freedom of human response.)[3] Both. And.

Methodist views of baptism express this "both/and" understanding. In the Confession of Faith (which came to United Methodism from the Evangelical United Brethren Church), baptism is described as "(signifying) entrance into the household of faith, and (as) a symbol of repentance and inner cleansing from sin, a representation of new birth in Christ Jesus and a mark of Christian discipleship."[4] Entrance into the household of faith? That sounds like an infant . . . or a youth or adult. Repentance? That sounds like a youth or adult. Both/And.

In fact, the Confession of Faith specifically names children as "acceptable subjects for Christian Baptism" because they "are under the atonement of Christ and . . . heirs of the Kingdom of God."[5, 6]

John Wesley wrote—in a sermon entitled "The Marks of the New Birth"—that being born again (born of the Spirit, child of God, born of God, having the Spirit of adoption) are "privileges, by the free mercy of God, (that) are ordinarily annexed to baptism" (John 3:5).[7] Yet the biblical truth is that we can sin away that grace given by God in baptism. That is why a person baptized as an infant later is called to make a personal profession of faith. That is why persons seek occasions to renew the baptismal covenant, not because God has changed God's mind but because we have not kept our end of the covenant: faithful discipleship. There is no occasion to baptize a second time (God is faithful), but there is frequent occasion for confession, repentance, profession, and renewal in order that we might let God's Spirit blow away the dust that has accumulated on our journey of faith. When that dust is gone, once again is revealed the unchanging mark "claimed by God in Jesus Christ."

In our baptism we put on Jesus Christ: "As many of you as were baptized in Christ have clothed yourselves with Christ" (Gal. 3:27). We have put on Christ's death, so in a sense we have already died. (There is no need to fear death now if we have already died!) But we have also put on Christ's resurrection, so in a sense we have already begun eternal life. (We are admitted into heaven not on our own ticket, but only if we present the ticket made valid by Jesus Christ.)

But, you ask, "How much water does it take to bring this off?" Not much. Or a lot. The water is a sign of the refreshing, cleansing power of the Holy Spirit, washing away sin and restoring to new life. Immersion (dunking the candidate completely under water) reminds us of our death to the old life and our emergence into new life (Rom. 6:3–5; Col. 2:12). Pouring (letting a large amount of water pour over the head of the candidate) reminds us of the flowing grace of God (Matt. 3:16; Mark 1:9–10). Sprinkling (a small amount of water on the head of the candidate) reminds us how the Holy Spirit descended on each head at Pentecost (Luke 3:21–22; Acts 2:38; 19:1–7). The mode of baptism (immersion, pouring, sprinkling) has varied from region to region and from time to time. Methodists acknowledge any of the three modes.[8]

> The mode of baptism (immersion, pouring, sprinkling) has varied from region to region and from time to time. Methodists acknowledge any of the three modes.

Methodists recognize water baptism in the name of the Father, and of the Son, and of the Holy Spirit, no matter the denominational setting for the baptism. Such a baptism is baptism into the entire Church of Jesus Christ. That means that a person who has, for example, been baptized in a Presbyterian church does not have to be baptized again when joining the United Methodist Church. A person who was baptized by immersion in a Baptist church would not be rebaptized when he or she becomes a member of the United Methodist Church. (Most Baptist congregations would, on the other hand, insist on baptizing by immersion any one who came to them without having previously been immersed.)

After several years of debate, United Methodists have come to accept baptized persons as full members of the United Methodist Church, no matter the age of that person. There is, however, a major distinction between baptized (full) members and professing members; those children who are full members are nurtured to make personal professions of faith. They then become professing members.

Baptism in the Wesleyan tradition is Trinitarian; that is, baptism is in the name of the Father, and of the Son, and the Holy Spirit.[9] This reality is called the Trinity.

(Unfortunately, at this moment I am reminded of the account of a man who said he would give his right arm to be ambidextrous. Hang on—there's a reason that story came to mind . . . I mean a reason other than the state of my mental well-being. Obviously, to take away the arm is to take away the ability to be ambidextrous. The one God exists in three persons—Father, Son, Holy Spirit. To diminish or take away any one of these three persons is to take away who God is.)

At the heart of the mystery of one God being three persons is the reality that God exists in community, in relationship. Father and Son talk to each other. The Holy Spirit proceeds from the Father and the Son. The Spirit brings the Son into the present. Yet there is only one God.[10]

Justo González suggests that Christians make a basic mistake of approaching the Trinity as a puzzle to be solved rather than an example to be imitated.[11] What is to be imitated? Community. Relationship. Unity.

The word "Trinity" does not appear in the Bible. The word was first used around 180 by Theophilus of Antioch. A couple of hundred years later, the Church was defending the teaching about the Trinity so that the Council of Nicea in 325 made the Trinity a centerpiece of classical Christian teaching.[12]

Although the word "Trinity" is not a biblical term, the truth of the Trinity is solidly biblical. Mark 14:36, Luke 23:46, and 1 Corinthians 8:6 all point to God the Father. Romans 10:9, Acts 2:36, and John 1:14 all point to God the Son. Acts 1:8, John 14:16, and Romans 8:14 all point to God the Holy Spirit. Galatians 4:6, Matthew 28:19, and John 14:16 all point to these three persons in relationship as one God.

The language sometimes used to describe this unity is "the three persons of the Godhead are of one substance." "Substance" comes from a Latin word meaning "to stand under." To be of one substance is to stand under the same essential nature, the same fundamental characteristic, the same quality. (That nature, characteristic, quality is love.)

Methodists baptize in the name of the Trinity (using the terms Father, Son, Holy Spirit) because the Trinity is the fullness of God. The Trinity is the community of God. That is why it is tragic and unbearable for our relationships to be broken; in that brokenness, we no longer reflect the image of God.

The classic terms for God are Father, Son, and Holy Spirit. Some persons find the word "Father" a difficult word to use for God. Perhaps they have had an abusive father. Perhaps the term supports a male-dominated society. Perhaps the word makes God seem distant, far-off. These are legitimate concerns. God is not male, so why use a male term to name God?

All human language falls short of naming God. "Father" is often used to tell about God because Jesus used that term (for example, John 17:21: "As you, Father, are in me and I am in you"). "Father" is sometimes used so Christians can find a common speech to address God. "Father" is used because it is a personal, relational term. ("Father" is a personal relationship, unlike "Creator," a term that describes not a personal relationship but a function of God.)

Methodists frequently use feminine images for God. Psalm 22:9 depicts God as a midwife who helps birth babies. Isaiah 42:14 says God is like a woman who is in labor as a baby is being born. Isaiah 49:15 suggests that God is like the mother who is nursing her baby. Isaiah 66:13 tells of God who comforts us as a mother comforts a child. Luke 15:8–10 depicts God as a woman who is searching for a lost coin. Matthew 23:37 gives an image of a mother hen who cares for her brood; God is like that. To fail to use some images of God that are feminine is to fail to tell the entire biblical story.[13]

The initiation (baptism) of persons, young and old, into the family of God (much as circumcision welcomed young boys into the Jewish faith community) is one of the sacraments of the Church, appointed by Christ and in which Christ is uniquely present, granting the gift of a means of grace. The water is an important symbol. (A sign points to something—"23 miles to Raleigh." A symbol participates in the reality to which it points; a national flag is respected in the same way as the country it represents is respected; it is a symbol because it does more than point to the country; it shares the meaning of what that country is.) Water is a symbol of the washing away of sin.

Taking away the power of sin is what God can do, God the Father, God the Son, God the Holy Spirit: the full experience of God.

This chapter on baptism and the Holy Trinity is pretty heavy sledding (or, if you don't live in snow country, pretty heavy slogging or pretty steep walking or pretty sandy strolling—well, you get the idea). Put this book under your pillow tonight to see if that helps. (It probably won't help, but at least you will be able to find it in the morning.)

What Are You Going to Do About It?

1. If you have been baptized, check with someone in your family to get the details of when, where, how, and by whom. Consider having a "Christian birthday" on the anniversary of your baptism.
2. When next there is to be a baptism at your church, ask the pastor about this idea: each family brings water from a lake, river, stream, or faucet near its home; that water is all put together to form the water from which the person will be baptized. This symbol would give the entire congregation a sense of responsibility for the nurture of the individual in the Christian faith.
3. Have your pastor (or some other missions leader) help you get in touch with missionaries who are serving in areas of the world that are largely non-Christian. Ask those missionaries what baptism means in those settings.
4. Write the definitive theological treatise on the Trinity. We shall all be grateful.

The Means

Suppose you have inadvertently locked your keys in the car. (Inadvertently? Come to think of it, you are not likely to do that on purpose!) How do you get to the keys? Perhaps you use a coat hanger to try to budge the door lock. Maybe you call a locksmith to use special tools to open the door. You could call home and ask your dear, sweet, understanding sister to drive fifteen miles to bring you the spare set of keys. It is possible that you could request the car dealer to make you a new key. Perhaps by chance you have used a magnet to hide an extra key under the front fender. (Note to any car thieves who happen to be reading this: I do not hide a key under the front fender of my car.) These are some ordinary ways of getting to those keys locked up inside.[1]

Of course, it is quite possible to use not-so-ordinary means to get into the car: a blowtorch to burn through the door; a small, well-placed stick of dynamite to open things up a bit; a crane to lift the car two hundred feet into the air and drop the car until the doors pop open. These ways might work, but they would not be ordinary.

No doubt you recognize how all this ties into John Wesley and Methodism!

John Wesley celebrated the fact that there are regular (ordinary) ways that God uses to give grace to us. God is by no means limited to these "ordinary means of grace," but the reflective life of the people of God reveals that there are channels most often used by God to provide needed grace. (If you want to brush up on "grace," look again at pages 5–6, 12–13; or, perhaps, reread all of the book up to this point; grace shows up over and over again: unmerited gift from God to do for us what we cannot do for ourselves.) God could use a blowtorch, but ordinarily does not!

Ordinary means of grace are the ways God chooses regularly to give grace. In a sermon preached in 1746,[2] Wesley wrote, "By 'means of grace' I understand outward signs, words, or actions ordained by God, and appointed for this end—to be the *ordinary* channels whereby [God] might convey to [humankind] preventing, justifying, and sanctifying grace."[3]

Methodist tradition acknowledges two categories of means of grace: instituted means of grace (works of piety) and prudential means of grace (works of mercy). This chapter focuses on the instituted means of grace. Chapter 8 includes a look at prudential means of grace.

A SIDE TRIP FOR A LITTLE BACKGROUND

The General Rules developed very early in Methodist history, 1739. The rules were set for the small groups (classes, societies) of Methodists who met to ensure mutual accountability, to work out their salvation, and to flee the judgment of God against sin. There was an expectation that persons who genuinely wanted to be delivered from their sins would show in their lives the fruit of salvation.

The rules were offered as ways to give evidence that one did indeed desire salvation. The three basic rules were (1) Do no harm; (2) Do good; and (3) Attend the ordinances of God. It is within the third basic rule that the early Methodists identified the ordinary means of God's grace.[4]

What are the ordinary means of grace, particularly as spelled out in the General Rules? The public worship of God. The ministry of the Word, either read or expounded. The Supper of the Lord. Family and private prayer. Searching the Scriptures. Fasting or abstinence.[5]

Wesley was quite clear that there was no inherent (or magical) power available in following these rules, "but that God alone is the giver of every good gift, the author of all grace; that the whole power is of him, whereby through any of these there is any blessing conveyed to our soul."[6]

A SIDE TRIP FOR A LITTLE BACKGROUND

Joyce could not believe her ears. Her longtime friend Dale was explaining how he thought it was okay to cheat on school exams. Dale explained, "God takes care of it."

"What!" screamed Joyce (somewhat surprised herself at the volume of her reply). "How can you claim that God takes care of it when you cheat! What about integrity? What about honesty? What about. . . ," she sputtered, "your common sense!"

Dale smiled and said, "I think it is like this. I go to church every Sunday. I read my Bible every day. I take Communion every time I can."

"So?"

"So, these are ways that God gives grace. Grace covers up sin. So, if I have enough grace stored up, my sin is taken care of."

Joyce covered her head with her hands. She knew that there was something wrong with this logic, but she just could not quite figure out what it was.[7]

Primary among the means of grace is the Lord's Supper. Sometimes Methodists call this sacrament Holy Communion; sometimes it is called Eucharist. A sacrament has these characteristics: Jesus Christ asked his followers to do it; there is some physical symbol; God has promised to give grace, to which the response is faith.

Some Christian traditions claim that the Lord's Supper is simply a human memorial (a remembering) of what God has done in the death of Jesus Christ. Other Christian traditions assert that the elements (bread and wine) are not just signs of the body and blood of Christ, but actually *become* the body and blood of Christ. As often is the case, Methodists get understanding from both of these views: there is a real presence of Jesus Christ in this sacrament, but it is a spiritual presence, not a bodily presence. Of course, it is nonetheless real for being spiritual![8]

> A sacrament has these characteristics: Jesus Christ asked his followers to do it; there is some physical symbol; God has promised to give grace, to which the response is faith.

There are many images of and dimensions to the Lord's Supper. Is it a family meal? Yes, it is a gathering at the family Table (1 Cor. 11:33). Is it partaking of the body and blood of Jesus? Yes, our Lord made this proclamation himself (Matt. 26:26–28). Is it an anticipation of God's full reign in the coming kingdom? Yes, it is an advance taste of the days God has planned for us (Luke 14:15). Is it a testimony to our Lord's death for us? Yes, it is the presence again of Jesus' sacrifice on the cross (1 Cor. 11:26). Is it witness to God's use of ordinary life to give extraordinary gifts? Yes, bread and wine are basic, daily food, but God touches them here with special grace (1 Cor. 11:23–24). Is it a way to remember Jesus? Yes, Christ's sacrifice was once for all, but commemorating that sacrifice is part of the Table (Heb. 7:27; Luke 22:19). Is it a fellowship of believers? Yes, there is a unity at the Lord's Table (1 Cor. 10:16–17). Is it a thanksgiving for what God has done in Christ? Yes, our Lord gave thanks and so do we (Mark 14:22–23). Is it a joyful occasion? Yes, although the Lord's Supper is about serious business, it is joyful business (Acts 2:46–47).

A SIDE TRIP FOR A LITTLE BACKGROUND

Antonio and Jerri met Lee at the front door of Holy Trinity Church. They had agreed to join Lee for the early morning Communion service at his church before the three of them left for a day at the beach. Although Antonio and Jerri were not members of Lee's church, the service seemed quite familiar. They felt right at home.

When it came time to receive the sacrament, the three friends stepped into the aisle and followed others to the front where the pastor was offering each one a bit of bread and a sip from the cup. ("We usually dip the bread in the cup," thought Jerri, "but I guess here they all drink from the common cup.") Lee went first, received the bread, and took a small sip from the chalice. Antonio was next. He swallowed the bread and put the silver goblet to his lips.

Antonio almost gagged. He began coughing and sputtering and, with great embarrassment, made his way back to the pew.

After the service he explained to his friends: "Wow! That stuff was wine, real wine! At my church we use grape juice. I guess my empty stomach was not expecting wine!"

Almost all congregations in the Methodist tradition use grape juice for Communion instead of wine. This practice is fairly recent, showing up in a *Book of Discipline* first in 1876. A dentist named Dr. Welch (recognize the name? grape juice? jelly?) was a Methodist layman who developed a way of preserving unfermented grape juice. His church began to use this juice, and soon many churches wanted to use it. Methodists have continued to use grape juice in large measure as part of its social witness against alcohol abuse, as pastoral support of those who cannot drink alcohol, and as a way to maintain a Table open to children and youth. (It seems common to the Methodist experience to blend worship and witness for social justice.) Just to make sure that this pattern of using grape juice for Communion was continued, the 1996 General Conference of the United Methodist Church passed a resolution (still in effect) that called for "the pure, unfermented juice of the grape" in this sacramental life.[9]

Some Christian denominations say that one must be a member of that tradition in order to come to the Lord's Table for Holy Communion. Other groups insist that one be a member of the congregation that is serving Communion. In some practices, one has to have made a profession of faith (be confirmed) in Jesus Christ in order to take Communion. Some groups have said one needed to have been immersed in order to be eligible for Holy Communion. Methodists offer what can be called "an open Table."[10]

Methodist practice has varied over the years. The Wesleys would have typically (but not always) followed the way of the Church of England in denying Communion to those not baptized. Early American Methodism sometimes closed the Communion Table to those not in good spiritual standing within their societies.[11] Today, a common pattern is to open the

Table to anyone who has been baptized (because baptism is understood to mean initiation into church membership). For pastoral and evangelical reasons, Methodists in the United States today seldom turn away anyone who comes to the Table. John Wesley even thought that conversion could take place at the Communion Table: "a converting ordinance."[12] It is the Lord's Table; we only seek to be good stewards of his invitation.

The Communion service uses these phrases: "Christ our Lord invites to his table all who love him, who earnestly repent of their sin and seek to live in peace with one another. Therefore, let us confess our sin before God and one another."[13] In truth, Methodists are not of one mind in interpreting this call to the Table.

John Wesley called for Methodist people to have frequent Communion. He asked that no Methodist preaching service be held at a time that conflicted with the Lord's Supper at the parish of the Church of England. He himself communed weekly, sometimes daily.[14] In American Methodism, the shortage of ordained clergy reduced the frequency of Communion. The people were delighted to have the regional supervisor come for the quarterly conference; they used the term "presiding elder" for the person in that office, not because these pastors presided at a business meeting, but because they presided at the Lord's Table. (Today, now that more persons are authorized to preside at the Table, United Methodists call these supervisors "district superintendents.")

How often do churches in your area have Communion? Methodist congregations are not all alike in the frequency of Communion. For some, once a quarter is the standard; others have the Lord's Supper on all special holy days; many congregations have monthly observances. For some denominations, Holy Communion is the regular service of worship each week. Increasing numbers of United Methodist congregations are offering this sacrament each week in some setting. The 2004 General Conference will receive a report encouraging weekly Communion in United Methodist churches.[15]

Because the Holy Communion is at its heart an event of the full Christian community, United Methodists are reminded that private observances of the Lord's Supper violate that central truth. For example, the *Book of Worship* says of Holy Communion at weddings, "Not only the husband and wife but the whole congregation are to be invited to receive communion."[16] When the sacrament is celebrated in hospital rooms or nursing homes, all Christians present are included in the invitation.[17]

A previous chapter spoke of two of the other means of grace: the ministry of the Word and searching the Scriptures (chapter 4). Preaching is a part of vital Methodism. (Remember that one of the definitions of the Church in the Articles of Religion of the Methodist Church is "a congregation of faithful [people] in which the pure Word of God is preached."[18]) Architecture has often reflected the importance of preaching as pulpits are placed in the center of worship space. (Other designs grow out of the varying emphases of what it means for the congregation to gather: to celebrate Communion, to be with one another in fellowship, to magnify Christ's sacrifice on the cross.) Some congregations in the Bible Belt refer to their main gathering space as the "auditorium." What is most valued in these settings is what is heard (audio-torium). Although faithful preaching is critical to the Methodist experience (for conversion, for social witness, for nurture, for rebuke, for vision, for teaching), it is not a Methodist tradition to call the chief worship space "auditorium."

> **Methodist congregations are not all alike in the frequency of Communion.**

A SIDE TRIP FOR A LITTLE BACKGROUND

HENRY: I can worship God at the park as I stroll alone.
SHERRIE: Hogwash.

God is at the park. God is with Henry when he strolls. But the call of this promise of God's grace is in the *public* worship of God.[19] Those worship settings will vary ("It is not necessary that rites and ceremonies should in all places be the same or exactly alike"[20]), but worship is communal and not a matter of private judgment.[21] Public worship affords accountability in the Christian journey. Public worship acknowledges that the faith walk is personal, but not private; it is communal, not isolated. Public worship admits that I need others. Public worship recognizes that the biblical account is of a God who most frequently calls and speaks through community. Public worship reminds us that worship is not judged simply by how it "makes me feel." Public worship is a celebration by the people God has called into being. Public worship is confession that we have broken the unity God has desired.[22] Public worship is reflective of biblical images of the faithful gathered together at God's throne in heaven.[23] No wonder that public worship is a means of grace![24] (Even so, maybe Sherrie—see above—could have been a bit kinder toward Henry!)

The means of grace include the public worship of God.

ANOTHER SIDE TRIP FOR A LITTLE MORE BACKGROUND

Jarrod circled the block for the third time. "We'll never get to the concert on time if we don't find a parking place," he moaned.

From the back seat, Angela said, "Let's ask Jesus to find us a parking place." She began to pray, "Oh, Lord, we need a place to put this car so we can get to the show on time. Help us. Amen."

John Wesley wrote that "prayer is the lifting up of the heart to God: all words of prayer without this are mere hypocrisy. Whenever therefore thou attemptest to pray, see that it be thy one design to commune with God, to lift thy heart to him, to pour out thy soul before him."[25] Corporate prayer and private prayer are means of grace. Prayer is not, however, an occasion of bringing God up to date on our needs. As John Wesley wrote, "So that the end of your praying is not to inform God, as though he knew not your wants already . . . not so much to move God . . . as to move yourselves, that you may be willing and ready to receive the good things he has prepared for you."[26]

Marjorie Suchocki, a United Methodist theologian, has said, "How God uses our prayers is up to God; our work is not to control what happens as a result of our praying, but to offer prayer faithfully for God to use as God can and will."[27] Prayer is a discipline, not done casually or trivially, but with openness to "Your will, not mine."[28]

Methodists frequently pray in unison printed prayers.[29] Sometimes these are written for special occasions; sometimes they are ancient prayers used by Christians for centuries. Praying aloud together creates community (or expresses the community that already exists). Not to draw upon prayers prayed by the faithful for centuries is what might be called "an arrogance of the contemporary." What a gift to be able to have our prayers join the saints of ages past!

Family prayer is specifically mentioned in the General Rules.[30] The early American Methodist circuit riders would be in a different home almost every night, but they always joined the family for prayer. It is difficult in today's fragmented and dispersed life to find common family time. Some families have simply agreed on a time when each one will pause for a moment of family prayer no matter where he or she might be scattered at that particular moment. At the throne of God's grace, the family is still together.

Fasting is a part of Methodist discipline. From the days of John Wesley, those who would be ordained in full connection have been asked, "Will you recommend fasting or abstinence, both by precept and example?"[31] Although Mr. Wesley outlined several reasons for fasting, he lifted up two as primary: (1) it helps in prayer, and (2) God commands it and rewards it.[32]

John Wesley's habit was to fast from sunrise until midafternoon on Wednesday and Friday.[33] Methodists have often lost that practice, a fact that caused Mr. Wesley to observe, "The man that never fasts is no more on the way to heaven than the man that never prays."[34] Ouch!

These means of grace (the public worship of God, the ministry of the Word, either read or expounded, the Supper of the Lord, family and private prayer, searching the Scriptures, fasting or abstinence) have been instituted by God in order to bless God's people. Thanks be to God!

What Are You Going to Do About It?

1. Find a friend in the faith who will help hold you accountable for being obedient to the means of grace.
2. Remind the planning group in your local church (perhaps the church council) to make sure it provides resources and settings that will help members keep the means of grace.
3. Get permission from somebody (your grandmother, perhaps?) to put up a bulletin board at the church. Use it for a series of displays on the means of grace.
4. Make a study of the hymnbook to find hymns that support the practice of the means of grace.
5. Find out where Communion is offered in your community and try to practice frequent Communion.

The Doing

A Methodist youth group went on a mission-building project in Jamaica. A Methodist group gathered at the state Capitol to protest the possibility of a state lottery. A Methodist pastor started small cell groups in her local church. A Methodist layperson made an impassioned speech against capital punishment. A Methodist organization offered a telephone prayer ministry. A Methodist Sunday School class went once a month to serve breakfast at a homeless shelter. A Methodist congregation hosted a neighborhood discussion of homosexuality. A Methodist teen told a friend he did not like it when his friend told racially demeaning jokes. A Methodist member got a five-hundred-dollar raise at work and immediately increased her church pledge by fifty dollars. A Methodist college sold the stock it owned in a company that made most of its money from the manufacture of alcoholic beverages.

What do all these things have in common? They are examples of Methodist doing, activity that is possible by God's sanctifying grace (grace that makes us holy). Methodist doing is about holiness, living a holy life, doing the things that reflect what it is to be a set-apart, holy people. It is the result of seeking always to focus fully on the love of God and the love of neighbor. Works of mercy are called prudential means of grace, meaning that over the centuries, Christians have discovered that God blesses such activity with grace. (It is "prudent," wise, to open oneself to such gifts from God, hence "prudential means of grace.")

For Methodists, holiness involves more than one's personal relationship with God. Holiness grows out of one's personal relationship with God, but it is social; that is, it involves others. In preaching on the Sermon on the Mount, John Wesley said, "Christianity is essentially a social religion, and . . . to turn it into a solitary religion is indeed to destroy it."[1] He also wrote, "The Gospel of Christ knows no religion but social, no holiness but social holiness."[2] The Christian walk is more than "just me and Jesus." It includes all those other folks whom Jesus loves and for whom Jesus died.

Methodists seek the sanctification (the holiness) of all that life touches. Colossians 1:17 is a recognition that Jesus Christ is Lord of all. God desires the whole, full life for all of God's creation, for all of God's created people. "God so loved the world . . ." (John 3:16), so we also must so love the world! The traditional language describing early American Methodism is "reform of the continent" and "spreading scriptural holiness over the land."[3]

For John Wesley, the big issues to be addressed were slavery, the poor, liquor traffic, prison reform, war, politics, and education.[4] Methodists have continued to think it is important to apply the freeing news of the gospel to bringing all humankind to freedom. (How to do this is often a matter of debate and even controversy. Hillary Rodham Clinton, George W. Bush, Dick Cheney, and John Edwards are all United Methodists, but they do not agree on the best approach to helping humankind.)

> For Methodists, holiness involves more than one's personal relationship with God. Holiness grows out of one's personal relationship with God, but it is social; that is, it involves others.

For almost one hundred years, groups that now form the United Methodist Church have stated principles for social justice. Such a document is now called "Social Principles" and is a part of *The Book of Discipline*. These statements are adopted by the General Conference every four years and represent the only official point of view of the denomination. (Of course, individuals and agencies of the church may speak on matters of social concern, but they do not speak in behalf of the entire Church; only the General Conference does that.)

"The Social Principles are a prayerful and thoughtful effort on the part of the General Conference to speak to the human issues in the contemporary world from a sound biblical and theological foundation as historically demonstrated in United Methodist traditions. They are intended to be instructive and persuasive in the best of the prophetic spirit. The Social Principles are a call to all members of the United Methodist Church to a prayerful, studied dialogue of faith and practice."[5]

A SIDE TRIP FOR A LITTLE BACKGROUND

It is tempting to plow into the long list of items approached in the Social Principles, but to do so is beyond the scope of this small book. The general categories are the Natural World, the Nurturing Community, the Social Community, the Economic Community, the Political Community, and the World Community.[6]

At its best, Methodism understands that the transformation of society is like all transformation, a gift of God's grace and not of human effort. The Methodist reputation for activism (busy, busy, busy) is largely well deserved, but its best expressions are responses to sanctifying grace.

In the Bible Belt (and in the suspenders mentality of other places!), there is often a plea not to mix religion and politics. Methodists see a Jesus who heals, who teaches, who forgives, who restores, and who is just, and they seek to be advocates of those systems that heal, that teach, that give new beginnings, that bring justice. There is enough sin in the human condition that official United Methodist positions dare not settle on any one partisan position as always right, but there is enough grace in God's saving activity in the world that Methodists dare not fail to see where God is at work and to join God in that work.

This work is nothing less than redemption of the whole created order.[7] The theological term for it is "entire sanctification," which means the full love of God and the full love of neighbor. Persons in the Wesleyan family use "Christian perfection" as another way of speaking of entire sanctification.

A SIDE TRIP FOR A LITTLE BACKGROUND

Perfect? Good grief, there is plenty of evidence that Methodists all around (including the one who types on this computer) fall far short of being perfect. John Wesley knew that the term "perfection" offended. So he sought (in his sermon "Christian Perfection") to teach what the term did *not* mean: freedom from ignorance, freedom from error, freedom from infirmities, freedom from temptations.[8] "Perfected Christians" are still bound by ignorance, error, infirmities, and temptation. They are perfect in their intent to love God and neighbor. It is a gift that God intends ("Be perfect, therefore, as your heavenly Father is perfect").[9] It is a call to complete love ("You shall love the Lord your God with all your heart, and with all your soul, and with all your strength, and with all your mind; and your neighbor as yourself").[10]

Candidates for ordination in full connection in the United Methodist Church are asked the same questions John Wesley asked his preachers: "Are you going on to perfection? Do you expect to be made perfect in love in this life? Are you earnestly striving after perfection in love?"[11] The appropriate response to each of these questions is "Yes."

This answer is not an ego trip. It is a statement of confidence in the fullness of God's grace. In contrast to some traditions, the Methodist energy is to see a connection between faith and holy living. Salvation is a journey both of faith and of holy living.

This kind of perfection is a maturity in love of God and neighbor. It is a completeness of love of God and neighbor. It is an entirety of love of God and neighbor. That is what it means to be holy. That is what it means to be perfect in love. The Christ in me is perfect in love![12]

A MUSICAL SIDE TRIP

Finish, then, thy new creation; pure and spotless let us be.
Let us see thy great salvation perfectly restored in thee;
changed from glory into glory, till in heaven we take our place,
till we cast our crowns before thee, lost in wonder, love, and praise.

(Charles Wesley[13])

The doctrinal heritage statement of the United Methodist Church includes these words: "New birth is the first step in this process of sanctification. Sanctification draws us toward the gift of Christian perfection, which Wesley described as a heart 'habitually filled with the love of God and neighbor' and as 'having the mind of Christ and walking as he walked.'"[14]

Methodists then understand that all their doing is not a way to earn some gift from God but a sign that God's gift of grace is already at work within God's people.

Methodists also believe that God's grace gives assurance to those in whose lives that grace is working. (Holy living is certainly one sign of that assurance.) Although John Wesley changed his mind from time to time, he most often felt that persons who were justified (saved from the power of sin) had assurance of that justification. Perhaps the most quoted words written by John Wesley are these words that describe his own experience of assurance:

In the evening [May 24, 1738], I went very unwillingly to a society in Aldersgate Street, where one was reading Luther's Preface to the Epistle to the Romans. About a quarter before nine, while he was describing the change which God works in the heart through faith in Christ, I felt my heart strangely warmed. I felt I did trust in Christ, Christ alone for salvation, and assurance was given me that he had taken away *my* sins, even *mine,* and saved *me* from the law of sin and death.[15]

(There are days I take comfort in the fact that Mr. Wesley went *unwillingly* to this Christian group meeting! He went even though he did not much want to and God still blessed him! I suppose I should remember that the next time the alarm clock goes off for an early Sunday service.)

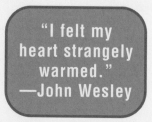

"I felt my heart strangely warmed." —John Wesley

This gift of assurance is understood to be the normal experience of folks who are justified by God's good grace. There are exceptions. Even someone as profoundly shaped by his spiritual experiences as John Wesley did not insist that everyone have exactly the same experience. One danger that sometimes gets loose in a Bible Belt culture is a narrow definition of what experiences with God look like. Ted A. Campbell has suggested that in a culture obsessed by sin, there would be great relief at the sense of deliverance. In a culture shaped more by a sense of directionless (such as this century), assurance might come in the form of a sense of direction.[16]

Methodist hymnwriter Fanny J. Crosby captured both the theme of perfection and the theme of assurance in this gospel song:

Blessed assurance, Jesus is mine! O what a foretaste of glory divine!
Heir of salvation, purchase of God, born of his Spirit, washed in his
    blood.
Perfect submission, all is at rest; I in my Savior am happy and blest;
watching and waiting, looking above, filled with his goodness, lost
    in his love.
This is my story, this is my song, praising my Savior all the day long;
this is my story, this is my song, praising my Savior all the day long.[17]

These two themes (perfection and assurance) are sometimes seen as distinctive Methodist contributions to the theological thought of the entire Christian family. This goal of perfection, holy living, and abundant life for all of God's creation drives Methodism to take the new life in Christ as a journey more than a destination.

Maybe Dwight L. Moody can give us a rack on which to hang this hat. He was an evangelist in the late nineteenth century. He said, "It's not how loud you shout or how high you jump; it's how straight you walk when you come down that counts."[18] (Personally, I plan to say that the next time I run into someone who wonders if Methodists have religion.)

What Are You Going to Do About It?

1. Have you written anything in your journal lately?
2. Go on-line and find some churches named "Aldersgate." E-mail them and ask how they got that name. Compare their answers with the wisdom given you in note 15 of this chapter.
3. Think of some issue or mission in which you have great interest. Consult with some Christian friends to see if this interest might be a call from God for you to take action. Read over the Social Principles (*The Book of Discipline, 2000,* 95–121) to get ideas.
4. Encourage your pastor to use the Social Creed in an occasional worship service. (It is on p. 122 of *The Book of Discipline, 2000.*) It is a summary of the Social Principles.

The Way

DAY ONE

METHODIST MARY: Hey, we're getting a new pastor. She moves here next week.

BIBLE BELT BILLY: A woman? Really? When did the congregation vote on her?

METHODIST MARY: Vote? The congregation does not vote on who will be the pastor. The bishop decides who the pastor will be.

BIBLE BELT BILLY: Gasp!

DAY TWO

BIBLE BELT BILLY: My daddy was just elected a deacon and was ordained last Sunday.

METHODIST MARY: Great! My dad was ordained deacon last week too! I guess we are the children of clergy now!

BIBLE BELT BILLY: What do you mean? My dad is a layman. He is a deacon, not the preacher.

METHODIST MARY: My dad is a deacon; that means that he is clergy.

BIBLE BELT BILLY: Gasp!

DAY THREE

METHODIST MARY: Did your church pay its apportionments this year?

BIBLE BELT BILLY: Our what?

METHODIST MARY: Apportionments. You know: money that you combine with other churches to send missionaries, build camps, open retirement homes, help homes for disadvantaged children, plan evangelism programs, employ staff to help local churches, support colleges, assist retired pastors, start new congregations, help with clergy continuing education, sponsor area youth ministry, give pastoral care, design spiritual formation settings, work for racial and gender inclusiveness, establish agencies for all kinds of ministries, and . . .

BIBLE BELT BILLY: Whoa! That's too much to process! My mental computer just shut down! What was the big word you used? Apportion—something.

METHODIST MARY: Apportionment. It's our local church share in all of those things. The annual conference decides what our share is. We always pay all of it. It does so much.

BIBLE BELT BILLY: We do some of those things, probably not all of them, but some of them. But nobody tells us how much to give. My church decides all that.

METHODIST MARY: How can your one church see the whole picture?

BIBLE BELT BILLY: Well, we see what we can.

METHODIST MARY: Gasp!

DAY FOUR

BIBLE BELT BILLY: My parents say I can't come to your church Sunday.

METHODIST MARY: I'm sorry you have a conflict.

BIBLE BELT BILLY: Well, there is no conflict on the calendar. They just don't think I should go to a church with a woman as pastor. They say the Bible says women should be submissive to men in spiritual things.

METHODIST MARY: Gasp!

DAY FIVE

METHODIST MARY: The district superintendent is coming to our church next Tuesday. It's time for charge conference.

BIBLE BELT BILLY: What is that?

METHODIST MARY: It's an official meeting for connecting us to all other United Methodist churches.

BIBLE BELT BILLY: How can you be sure they are all Bible-believing churches?

METHODIST MARY: One reason we are connected is to help each other discover God's will for all of us.

BIBLE BELT BILLY: And the district superintendent?

METHODIST MARY: He is an extension of the office of the bishop, the one who has oversight over a whole bunch of churches.

BIBLE BELT BILLY: Gasp!

These rather unlikely conversations do raise important issues. (Gasp! Where I come from, most folks don't carry on like this, but, hey, this is a book, not a taped message!) The issues are all about polity. Polity is the way a group organizes its life in order to get its mission done. Sometimes, polity is simply a matter of "what works." Sometimes, polity grows out of deeply held beliefs. Methodist polity is both.

Methodists are a connectional people. When one joins a local United Methodist Church, for example, one joins the entire denomination.[1] "Connectionalism in the United Methodist tradition is multi-leveled, global in scope, and local in thrust. Our connectionalism is not merely a linking of one charge conference to another. It is rather a vital web of interactive relationships."[2]

> Methodists are a connectional people. When one joins a local United Methodist Church, for example, one joins the entire denomination.

This way of organizing is both practically and theologically (biblically) rooted. It is practical because more can get done by working together than can get done by going it alone. It is theologically rooted in the biblical understanding that Church is community, not isolated pockets of believers.[3] Mr. Wesley did not think the Methodist way of organizing was the only biblical way to organize, but he was convinced that it was solidly in keeping with the New Testament Church. Further, he recognized good church order as what would get the job done: "What is the end of all ecclesiastical order? Is it not to bring souls from the power of Satan to God, and to build them up in his fear and love? Order, then, is so far valuable as it answers these ends; and if it answers them not, it is worth nothing."[4]

So, Methodist polity is not accidental. It is an important part of how Methodists define themselves, how Methodists embark themselves for mission, and how Methodists practice disciplined life as Christians. It is not a casual, doesn't-really-matter kind of thing. It is of the essence of being Methodist.[5]

The structure of United Methodism is a series of conferences. (The word "conference" comes from "confer," which is a word suggesting connection, conversation, mutual accountability, and relationship—no wonder "conferencing" is considered a means of grace!)

Charge Conference: At the local level, there is a charge conference.[6] The pastor is the administrative officer.[7]

District Conference: Several churches (usually forty to seventy-five) in one area form a district that can meet from time to time as a district conference.[8]

Annual Conference: The larger regional area forms an annual conference (guess how often it meets).[9] The annual conference is the basic body of the United Methodist Church.[10] (At the annual conference, persons are elected for ordination, Constitutional amendments are voted on, delegates are selected who will choose the bishops, delegates are elected who will vote on *The Book of Discipline*, and decisions are made about how congregation will share financially—apportionments—in expenditures for connectional ministries.) Although bishops are bishops of the whole Church, they are assigned to work in specific annual conferences.[11]

Jurisdictional Conference: Then, in the United States there are five jurisdictional conferences, each one having boundaries that take in several states.[12] (Outside the United States, these larger bodies are called central conferences.[13]) Annual conferences elect clergy and lay delegates to these jurisdictional or central conferences. Their main work is the election of bishops.[14]

General Conference: The annual conferences elect delegates to General Conference, which is the worldwide legislative body for the United Methodist Church.[15] This group determines the content of *The Book of Discipline* (with six constitutional limitations).[16]

This connection of conferences has its roots in a 1744 meeting when John Wesley called together preachers who were in connection with him.

He wrote, "This I did for many years, and all that time the term *conference* meant not so much the conversations we had together, as the persons that conferred."[17] The task of those Wesleyan conferences was to determine "(1) what to teach, (2) how to teach, and (3) what to do; that is how to regulate our doctrine, discipline, and practice."[18] In large measure, these remain the agenda when Methodists gather as conference.

The General Conference forms a legislative branch of United Methodist structure. The bishops form an executive branch. There is also a judicial branch called the Judicial Council. Balancing these three ingredients in United Methodist life is important and recognizes that power should not accumulate into any one place. (A theology that includes sin is bound to acknowledge the need to keep power from falling in one place!)[19]

Non-Methodists are often puzzled by the Methodist practice of having the clergy appointed by the bishops. After consultation with others,[20] the resident bishop assigns pastors to their appointments for the next year. This system is rooted in the New Testament concept of *episcopas*, a word meaning "overseer," one who has oversight. (We translate the word as "episcopal" or "bishop.") The best decisions are made by those who can see the whole picture rather than by those who have a more limited view. All of this is the gift of the Holy Spirit.[21] The mission of the movement is the prime criterion by which the best decisions are made. What about the plan of deciding pastoral assignments on a year-by-year basis? What about the system that means all preachers are subject to being moved; in other words, what about the itinerant system?

Moving pastors from place to place is Methodism's commitment to deploy personnel in the way that does the most good in keeping with the ministry of making disciples of Jesus Christ. Those clergy who are elders in full connection agree to go wherever sent; in exchange, the conference assures those in good standing that they shall have an appointment. (The annual conference determines who is to be appointed; the bishop and district superintendents decide where each one is appointed. Again, note that there is a balance of power.) In a letter to Samuel Walker in 1756, John Wesley penned, "We have found by long and constant experience that a frequent change of preachers is best. This preacher has one talent, that another. No one whom I ever yet knew has all the talents which are needful for beginning, continuing, and perfecting the work of grace in an whole congregation."[22]

Itinerancy is a plan that works as an expression of Methodism as a connection. More than a collection of independent congregations, Methodist churches exist as expressions of a connection. One way to say it is "Decisions are not what is best for *me*; they are what is best for *us*."

Who are these clergy? Elders are those ordained for Word, order, sacrament, and service. (They usually serve as pastors of local congregations or in extension ministry as teachers, counselors, administrators. They are authorized "to preach and teach the Word of God, to administer the sacraments of baptism and Holy Communion, and to order the life of the Church for mission and ministry."[23]) Deacons are those ordained for servant leadership and for connecting Church and world. (They sometimes serve on staff of local churches and often have ministries in the community: teachers, counselors, mission coordinators. They are eligible to conduct marriages and to bury the dead and to assist elders in the sacraments.[24]) In addition, the United Methodist Church recognizes local pastors, laypersons who are appointed to serve as pastors of local churches and who have sacramental authority only in the place to which they are appointed.[25] (Do you enjoy confusing people? Try this: in the United Methodist Church the pastor of a local church might not be a local pastor, but a local pastor is the pastor of a local church. Try saying that fast three times! The trick is that the pastor of a local church might be an elder; "local pastor" is a term used only to describe laypersons who have been licensed to be pastors of local churches! If you find yourself unable to sleep tonight because of this conundrum, wait until about 5:00 A.M. and then call your nearest district superintendent and ask him or her to explain it.)

Him or her? United Methodists have both men and women who serve as pastors, as district superintendents, and as bishops. Some Bible Belt churches do not allow women to become clergy, and their members even refuse to attend churches that have women pastors. Often, these attitudes are based on 1 Corinthians 11:2–16 and 1 Corinthians 14:34–35, passages in which Paul speaks to specific problems that had emerged in one congregation (Corinth) and in which Paul draws on cultural hairstyles to try to find a solution to the problem. To deny women the right to hear and respond to God's call to ordination and to deny the Church's authority in Christ to confirm that call is to miss the thrust of the New Testament Church's life: women prayed and prophesied in church (1 Cor. 11:5); women were leaders in the church (Euodia, Syntyche, Mary, Prisca,

Tryphosa, Junia, Tryphaena, Lydia, Dorcas, for example); women were set apart as deacons (Phoebe). John Wesley noted in his commentary on 1 Corinthians 11:11, "Neither [male nor female] is excluded; neither is preferred before the other in [God's] Kingdom."[26] Galatians 3:28 reinforces this view: ". . . there is no longer male and female; for all of you are one in Christ Jesus."[27]

John Wesley understood that churches in the times of the apostles had "different customs in things that were not essential."[28] Methodists try to make that distinction between those things that are essential and those things that are not essential. General Conference meets every four years and makes adjustments on those things determined not to be essential. Things can simply be made to work better. Disagreements, strong disagreements, however, emerge when equally faithful people do not agree on what is essential.[29]

> To deny women the right to hear and respond to God's call to ordination and to deny the Church's authority in Christ to confirm that call is to miss the thrust of the New Testament Church's life.

Because the United Methodist Church is connectional (see para. 139 in *The Book of Discipline*), the title to all church property is held in trust for the United Methodist Church.[30] This concept grows out of John Wesley's desire to protect Methodist property from takeover by those who did not maintain Methodist doctrine and practice. The conference in England developed a "model deed" which assured that only those in connection with Mr. Wesley controlled use of these buildings. American Methodism adopted the same practice and included a "trust clause" in early editions of *The Book of Discipline*. This clause still exists. It does not mean that the denomination owns the property; the local church owns the property in agreement to operate it under the provisions of *The Book of Discipline*. Anyone who gives money to build a United Methodist building knows that the building or proceeds from its sale will always be for the ministry of the United Methodist Church. The clause says,

> In trust, that said premises shall be used, kept, and maintained as a place of divine worship of the United Methodist ministry and

members of The United Methodist Church; subject to the *Discipline*, usage and ministerial appointments of said Church as from time to time authorized and declared by the General Conference and by the annual conference within whose bounds the said premises are situated. This provision is solely for the benefit of the grantee and the grantor reserves no right or interest in said premises.[31]

That is legal talk for "we are all in this together." Connection, Conference, Covenant. United Methodists have a Constitution[32] and a Judicial Council to decide when legislation in *The Book of Discipline* violates that Constitution. The organization is filled with balance, all of which is intended to make most likely fulfillment of the mission of making disciples of Jesus Christ. Sometimes it works; sometimes it doesn't. Always God does.

What Are You Going to Do About It?

1. Attend a meeting of your local church's decision-making group (perhaps a "church council").
2. Find out when the annual conference will meet again and see if a carload might go spend a day at this gathering.
3. Review *The Book of Discipline* and find some portions that you think need to be changed. Any member of a United Methodist church can petition General Conference to make a change. Go on the United Methodist website to find out how to do it: www.umc.org.
4. Ask your pastor how persons are elected to be delegates to jurisdictional and general conferences. If you feel called of God to be such a delegate, give it a try!

The Others

When the Apostles' Creed (recognized around 400) and the Nicene Creed (written in 325) appear in the *United Methodist Hymnal,* there is an asterisk next to the word "catholic." "We believe in the one holy catholic* and apostolic church," "I believe in the Holy Spirit, the holy catholic* church." At the bottom of the page, the asterisk is explained: "catholic" means "universal."[1] This comment was added because some persons feared that worshipers would think that the word "catholic" meant the Roman Catholic Church. In these creeds, "catholic church" means God's universal Church throughout the world, in all flavors and names.

How do Methodists relate to persons of other Christian traditions? How do Methodists relate to persons of non-Christian faiths? How do Methodists relate to persons who claim no faith?

Let's approach the topic as one might pick up a porcupine: carefully. On the one hand, the central, driving mission of Methodism is to make disciples of Jesus Christ. On the other hand, Methodists are fully aware that God has dreams and visions that reach far beyond our human grasp. On the one hand, the gospel is clear that the way to God is through Jesus Christ.[2] On the other hand, the gospel is clear that Jesus knows of some sheep we might not recognize as part of the flock.[3] On the one hand, Methodists seek to be faithful to God's call; on the other, Methodists recognize apostolic truth and practice in other traditions.

Methodists hold basic Christian affirmations in common with other Christian communions. These beliefs include having faith in the mystery of salvation through Jesus Christ, acknowledging the activity of the Holy Spirit in human life, sharing in a universal Church, recognizing God's reign now and in the future, and seeing the authority of Scripture.[4]

> "Ecumenical" means the whole inhabited world, literally the whole house. "Economy" means the management of the whole house. God's economy is how God manages the world.

Because of Methodists' awareness that God's grace exceeds any boundary established by humankind, Methodists have been a part of the major expressions of ecumenical Christianity: Churches Uniting in Christ, National Council of Churches, World Council of Churches, World Methodist Council, Commission on Pan-Methodist Cooperation (United Methodist, AME Church, AMEZ Church, CME Church), National Association of Evangelicals, World Evangelical Fellowship,[5] and the newly emerging Christian Churches Together in the U.S.A. In *Explanatory Notes upon the New Testament*, John Wesley commented on Jesus' prayer in John 17:11 that "they may all be one": "*that they may be one*—With [the Trinity], and with each other: one body, separate from the world."[6]

A word often used to describe this oneness is "ecumenism." Notice in the word the same source as in the word "economy." "Ecumenical" means the whole inhabited world, literally the whole house. "Economy" means the management of the whole house. God's economy is how God manages the world. Ecumenical movements are efforts to reflect how God brings unity from diversity.

In his sermon "Catholic Spirit," John Wesley draws on a text from 2 Kings 10:15: "And when he was departed thence, he lighted on Jehonadab the son of Rechab *coming* to meet him; and he saluted him and said to him, 'Is thine heart right, as my heart *is* with thy heart? And Jehonadab answered, It is. If it be, give *me* thine hand.'"

Although Wesley might have fudged a bit on the context of that verse (it has to do with agreeing to slay enemies), he drew from the phrase helpful conclusions. Does catholic spirit mean "give me your hand if you have the same opinion as I do"? No. Does catholic spirit mean "give me your hand if you worship in the same mode as I do"? No. Does catholic spirit mean "I am unsure about what I believe"? No.

The catholic spirit to which the Methodist family is called is to be one whose "heart is enlarged toward all (humankind), those (one) knows and those (one) does not; one embraces with strong and cordial affection neighbours and strangers, friends and enemies."[7]

A SIDE TRIP FOR A LITTLE BACKGROUND

John Wesley lived in a time when there was great animosity, politically and religiously, against Roman Catholics. The memory lingered of the bitter battles between Roman Catholics and Protestants for rights to the throne. In the midst of that acrimony, Wesley wrote "A Letter to a Roman Catholic."

"In the name, then, and in the strength of God, let us resolve, first, not to hurt one another; to do nothing unkind or unfriendly to each other, nothing which we would not have done to ourselves. . . . Let us resolve, secondly, God being our helper, to speak nothing harsh or unkind of each other. The sure way to avoid this is to say all the good we can both of and to one another. . . . Let us, thirdly, resolve to harbour no unkind thought, no unfriendly temper, towards each other. . . . Let us, fourthly, endeavour to help each other on in whatever we are agreed leads to the kingdom."[8]

In Methodist heritage, there is no invitation to do mean-spirited attacks against those with whom we disagree. This is not to say that Methodists do not sometimes slip into their shadow selves and do unkind things, say unfair things, and abuse others spiritually. When Methodists are at their best, their spirit is of love, even when the tone of love is corrective or challenging.

It is one thing to join other Christians in services of worship, to team up with other Christians in work projects, and to enjoy fellowship with other Christians in study. How do Methodists relate to persons who are not Christian?

In creating a General (denomination-wide) Commission on Christian Unity and Interreligious Concerns, *The Book of Discipline, 2000* spells out one of the purposes: "To advocate and work for the establishment and strengthening of relationships with other living faith communities, and to further dialogue with persons of other faiths, cultures, and ideologies."[9] The balance is between being neighbor and being witness. The ingredient of the relationship is always love.[10]

The 2000 General Conference of The United Methodist Church, well before the events of September 11, 2001, raised sensitivity to relationships between Muslims and Christians, amended and readopted a 1988 resolution opposing "demagoguery, manipulation, and image making that seeks to label Arabs and Muslims in a negative way."[11] In addition, the General Conference left in place a 1992 resolution that used the story of the good Samaritan (Luke 10:25–37) to challenge United Methodists to be hospitable neighbors to the strangers of other faiths, as the Samaritan showed compassion on someone of another faith. The statement says, "When Christians enter dialogue (with Muslims), they come to it consciously as they seek to live as one people, under the living God who is the Creator of all humankind, the One 'who is above all and through all and in all'" (Eph. 4:6).[12] The Social Principles state a minimal standard: "We assert the right of all religions and their adherents to freedom from legal, economic, and social discrimination."[13]

A SIDE TRIP FOR A LITTLE BACKGROUND

John Wesley, no slouch when it came to defending vigorously the truth of the Christian gospel, wrote "A Caution Against Bigotry." He recognized that there were many points of common life where all faiths might work together to achieve things for God. He said, "Yea, if it could be supposed that I should see a Jew, a deist, or a Turk (Muslim) doing the same thing, were I to forbid him either directly or indirectly I should be no better than a bigot still."[14]

The Scriptures provide a very broad background against which to paint Christian attitudes toward non-Christians. "I am the way, and the truth, and the life. No one comes to the Father except through me" (John 14:6). But then it says, "Then Peter began to speak to them: 'I truly understand that God shows no partiality, but in every nation anyone who fears [God] and does what is right is acceptable to [God]'" (Acts 10:34–35).

Methodists are a people who value experience.

On the other hand, "There is salvation in no one else, for there is no other name under heaven given among mortals by which we must be saved" (Acts 4:12). Then, there is this story: "John answered, 'Master, we saw someone casting out demons in your name, and we tried to stop him, because he does not follow with us.' But Jesus said to him, 'Do not stop him; for whoever is not against you is for you" (Luke 9:49–50). Methodist passion for witnessing to the saving power of Jesus Christ is unleashed through a filter of grace which knows that God's ways are not our ways and that God is able to do far more abundantly than we can imagine. God is quite capable of sorting out all these religions!

John Wesley had unblemished intent in evangelizing for Jesus Christ. Nevertheless, his notes on Acts 10:35 demonstrate how he understood this in relation to persons of other faiths (the translation is Wesley's own):

> *But in every nation he that feareth him, and worketh righteousness*— He that first reverences God, as great, wise, good: the Cause, End, and Governor of all things; and, secondly, from this awful regard to Him, not only avoids all known evil, but endeavours, according to the best lights he has, to do all things well. *Is accepted of him*— Through Christ, though he knows Him not. The assertion is express and admits of no exception. He is in the favour of God, whether enjoying His written word and ordinances or not.[15]

Methodists are a people who value experience. They value and celebrate experiences with Jesus Christ. They seek to live lives that show that Jesus Christ has engaged them in personal relationships. They work to let all the world and the world's people begin to reflect God's intent for a just and loving society. And they want others—all others—to experience Jesus Christ, so they sing,

Spirit of faith, come down, reveal the things of God,
and make to us the Godhead known, and witness with the blood.
'Tis thine the blood to apply and give us eyes to see,
who did for every sinner die hath surely died for me.

No one can truly say that Jesus is the Lord,
unless thou take the veil away and breathe the living Word.
Then, only then, we feel our interest in his blood,
and cry with joy unspeakable, "Thou art my Lord, my God."

O that the world might know the all-atoning Lamb!
Spirit of faith, descend and show the virtue of his name;
the grace which all may find, the saving power, impart,
and testify to humankind, and speak in every heart.

Inspire the living faith (which whosoe'er receive,
the witness in themselves they have and consciously believe),
the faith that conquers all, and doth the mountain move,
and saves who'er on Jesus call, and perfects them in love.

(Charles Wesley[16])

What Are You Going to Do About It?

1. Find a trusted Christian friend and talk about your own personal relationship with Jesus Christ.
2. Start a list of friends and family who do not acknowledge Jesus Christ as their Lord and Savior. Pray over the list daily and begin to think of ways you could tell them about your own faith journey. (Most faith journeys include stumbles and starts, valleys and mountains, dogs and cats. Okay, I'm not sure about that last one, but it just sort of flowed out of my keyboard. Don't blame me.)
3. Spend some time visiting the faith communities of friends of yours. Try to learn how God has reached them in their setting.
4. Put the book down and go take a nap. If anyone complains about it, tell them that I told you to do it.

Notes

INTRODUCTION

1. *The Book of Discipline of The United Methodist Church, 2000* (Nashville: United Methodist Publishing House, 2000), part 3, section 1, paragraph 120.

2. If you find your appetite for this kind of reading irresistibly whetted, you can borrow *The Book of Discipline* from any United Methodist pastor or buy one from Cokesbury (1-800-672-1789).

3. *The Book of Discipline of The United Methodist Church, 2000*, part 1, section 3, paragraph 16.

4. Three good places to read about this discussion among Wesleyan scholars are: Thomas C. Oden, *Doctrinal Standards in the Wesleyan Tradition* (Grand Rapids, Francis Asbury Press of Zondervan Publishing House, 1988); Richard P. Heitzenrater, "At Full Liberty: Doctrinal Standards in Early American Methodism," in Thomas A. Langford, ed., *Doctrine and Theology in The United Methodist Church* (Nashville: Kingswood Books of Abingdon Press, 1991); and Scott J. Jones, *United Methodist Doctrine* (Nashville: Abingdon Press, 2002).

5. *The Book of Discipline of The United Methodist Church, 2000*, chapter 7, section 2, paragraph 2702.

6. For example, the immensely popular "Left Behind" series of books (over 50,000,000 sold) has generated a wide range of resources on the rapture, including a web site with daily devotions, trivia from the books, prizes, and a newsletter. Although some Methodists have been attracted to this outburst of stories about the

"rapture," the doctrine itself has no place in Methodist theology. Indeed, it assumes a reading of Scripture that most Methodist theologians would find frail at best and faulty at worst.

CHAPTER 1. THE HOUSE

1. Rupert E. Davies, ed., *The Works of John Wesley,* vol. 9 (Nashville: Abingdon Press, 1989), 227.

2. *United Methodist Hymnal* (Nashville: United Methodist Publishing House, 1989), viii–ix.

CHAPTER 2. THE OOPS

1. As I was typing these words, I paused to check my horoscope on several Internet sites. To put it kindly, the astrology authorities do not seem to agree on my fate for today. The seven astrologists I checked (there are tons of such sites in an assortment of languages) reported that (1) I hate to have others whispering behind my back; (2) I could get career success by traveling; (3) I should cooperate with my friends; (4) I should refuse to let others put demands on me; (5) I show much promise for love and fun; (6) I should go with the flow; (7) love in my life could be upset in a few days by a twist. (I would have read more but I was too busy making plans for enriching travel for love and fun that would lead friends with whom I had been cooperating to talk about me behind my back.)

2. "We believe, however, [a human being] influenced and empowered by the Holy Spirit, is responsible in freedom to exercise his [or her] will for good" (article 7, "The Confession of Faith of the Evangelical United Brethren Church," paragraph 103, section 3, *The Book of Discipline of The United Methodist Church, 2000*).

3. Most persons in the Bible Belt do not accept astrology. Horoscopes, however, are often a part of popular culture, printed in daily newspapers and on numerous web sites. Whether it is for entertainment value or for serious life planning, astrology is outside the pale of good science and good religion.

4. "Water, air, soil, minerals, energy resources, plants, animal life, and space are to be valued because they are God's creation" (paragraph 160, "Social Principles," *The Book of Discipline of The United Methodist Church, 2000*).

5. Gen. 1:26–27.

6. Okay, I cannot resist. There is a story—probably not true—about a college that prided itself on high morals and strict discipline. Its catalog is reputed to have included this phrase: "Our campus is fourteen miles from the nearest known sin." (Well-informed locals could have spotted something a bit closer!)

7. "Original sin standeth not in the following of Adam (as the Pelagians do vainly talk), but it is the corruption of the nature of every [one], that naturally is engendered of the offspring of Adam, whereby [humankind] is very far gone from original righteousness, and of his own nature inclined to evil, and that continually" (paragraph 103, section 3, article 7, "The Articles of Religion of the Methodist Church," *The Book of Discipline of The United Methodist Church, 2000*).

8. Persons in many fields of study have noticed that "sin" has fallen out of public conversation. Over a generation ago, a prominent psychiatrist, Karl Menninger, wrote a book titled *Whatever Became of Sin?* (New York: Hawthorn Books, 1973).

9. In John Wesley's *Explanatory Notes upon the New Testament*, the founder of the Methodist movement commented on this passage: "That all . . . are under sin appears from the vices which have raged in all ages. . . . *There is none righteous*. This is the general proposition. The particulars follow: their dispositions and designs, verses 11–2; their discourses, verses 13–4; their actions, verses 16–8." John Wesley, *Explanatory Notes upon the New Testament* (Naperville, Ill.: Alec R. Allenson, 1958), 528.

10. If you cannot sleep tonight without knowing more about this, open the window and shout for someone to bring you a copy of *John Wesley's Message Today*, by Lovett H. Weems Jr. (Nashville: Abingdon Press, 1991).

11. "The condition of man after the fall of Adam is such that he cannot turn and prepare himself, by his own natural strength and works, to faith, and calling upon God; wherefore we have no power to do good works, pleasant and acceptable to God, without the grace of God by Christ preventing (going before) us, that we may have a good will, and working with us, when we have that good will." Paragraph 103, section 3, article 8, "The Articles of Religion of the Methodist Church," *The Book of Discipline of The United Methodist Church, 2000*.

12. Albert C. Outler, ed., *The Works of John Wesley*, vol. 2 (Nashville: Abingdon Press, 1985), 157.

13. Ibid., 156.

14. To get some help for inviting others to a relationship with Jesus Christ, contact the Section on Evangelism, the General Board of Discipleship of The United Methodist Church, Post Office Box 34003, Nashville, Tennessee 37203-0003.

CHAPTER 3. THE PEOPLE

1. Understand that I would never suggest that you do this: if you have a friend who seems, shall we say, a bit overconfident about biblical knowledge, ask him or her to read aloud Neh. 10:1–27. This list is one of the more challenging group of names! Malchijah? Magpiash? Pahath-moab?

2. Albert Outler, ed., *The Works of John Wesley,* vol. 1 (Nashville: Abingdon Press, 1984), 533.

3. "Connexion" is the British spelling for "connection." Not that you asked, but Toni and I named our retirement home "Connexion."

4. Elizabeth A. Livingstone, ed., *The Concise Oxford Dictionary of the Christian Church* (London: Oxford University Press, 1977), 204.

5. Article 1 of the Articles of Religion—Of Faith in the Holy Trinity: "There is but one living and true God, everlasting, without body or parts, of infinite power, wisdom, and goodness; the maker and preserver of all things, both visible and invisible. And in unity of this Godhead there are three persons, of one substance, power, and eternity—the Father, the Son, and the Holy Ghost" (*Book of Discipline of The United Methodist Church, 2000,* part 2, section 3, paragraph 103, article 1, 59).

6. *The Book of Discipline of The United Methodist Church, 2000,* part 2, section 3, paragraph 103, article 5, 67.

7. Eph. 2:14.

8. Gal. 3:26–28.

9. Eph. 5:23–24.

10. John 17:20–21.

11. 1 Peter 2:9.

12. Acts 2:42.

13. Eph. 2:19.

14. 1 Thess. 1:2–5.

15. Luke 11:28; John 1:14.

16. Col. 1:25–26.

17. Rom. 6:3; 1 Cor. 11:26.

18. Matt. 28:19; 26:26–29.

19. 1 Cor. 12:3.

20. Rev. 19:10.

21. Eph. 4:11–13.

22. Col. 1:18–20.

23. 2 Cor. 5:1.

24. 2 Cor. 4:7.

CHAPTER 4. THE BOOK

1. Ha! You thought I'd tell you what this word means! My eighth-grade English teacher, Ms. Smith, told me, "It will mean more to you if you look it up for yourself." Who am I to challenge Ms. Smith?

2. Quoted in Wesley D. Camp, *Word Lover's Book of Unfamiliar Quotations* (Paramus, N.J.: Prentice Hall, 1990), 23.

3. In his sermon "On Predestination," John Wesley describes the route to heaven: "(1) God knows all believers; (2) wills that they should be saved from sin; (3) to that end justifies them; (4) sanctifies; and (5) takes them to glory" (Albert Outler, ed., *The Works of John Wesley,* vol. 2 [Nashville: Abingdon, 1985], 421).

4. Outler, ed., *The Works of John Wesley,* vol. 1, 105.

5. About fifty years ago, an Englishman, J. B. Phillips, published books (The Macmillan Company) which set out to put the New Testament into easy-to-read English. A few wags—I was not included, of course—said that if Dr. Phillips did a paraphrase of the entire Bible, it could be called "Phillips' 66."

6. "The Holy Scripture containeth all things necessary to salvation; so that whatsoever is not read therein, nor maybe proved thereby, is not to be required of any [person] that it should be believed as an article of faith, or be thought requisite or necessary to salvation." *The Book of Discipline of The United Methodist Church, 2000,* part 2, paragraph 103, section 3, article 5, "Of the Sufficiency of the Holy Scripture for Salvation," 60.

7. Want to know more? Read article 6 ("Of the Old Testament") in *The Book of Discipline of The United Methodist Church, 2000,* 61.

8. Although the statement "Our Theological Task" does not carry the authority of the doctrinal standards, it does reflect a contemporary effort by United Methodists to deal with taking theology (talk about God) seriously. The full declaration can be found in *The Book of Discipline of The United Methodist Church, 2000,* 74–86.

9. Outler, ed., *The Works of John Wesley,* vol. 1, 104.

10. Ibid., 105–6.

11. If you want to dig a little deeper into Methodist approaches to biblical study, check out *How United Methodists Study Scripture,* ed. Gayle C. Felton (Nashville: Abingdon Press, 1999). It is a book I wish I had written!

12. *The Journal and Letters of Francis Asbury,* ed. Elmer T. Clark (Nashville: Abingdon Press, 1958), I: 311.

CHAPTER 5. THE GUIDE

1. *ESPN the Magazine Presents Answer Guy 2003 Calendar* (Kansas City, Mo.: Andrews McMeel Publishing, 2003).

2. "Adverse Camber" is the term used on British road signs to indicate that there is a dangerous arch in a highway. It has very little to do with this discussion,

but ever since I saw one of those signs, I have wanted to work it into something I wrote. Mission accomplished.

3. W. Stephen Gunter, ed., *Wesley and the Quadrilateral* (Nashville: Abingdon Press, 1997), 10.

4. "Quadrilateral" was used in an interim report published in 1970, but the term was not part of the statement adopted in 1972 (ibid., 10).

5. One arena in which this emphasis on experience (feeling) is played out is how the Christian community should worship. Is worship simply addressed to God or is worship defined by how worshipers feel? For a healthy discussion of these dimensions in worship, read Marva J. Dawn, *Reaching Out Without Dumbing Down* (Grand Rapids: Wm. B. Eerdman Publishing Co., 1995).

6. Outler, ed., *The Works of John Wesley*, vol. 1, 397.

7. *United Methodist Hymnal* (Nashville: United Methodist Publishing House, 1989), 372.

8. Thank Goodness, the name "Methodists" stuck. Otherwise, the title of this book might be *Being Bible Moths in the Bible Belt.*

9. *The Book of Discipline, 2000*, para. 104, 78.

10. Rebekah L. Miles develops this thought in Gunter, ed., *Wesley and the Quadrilateral*, 78.

11. W. Reginald Ward, ed., *The Works of John Wesley,* vol. 20 (Nashville: Abingdon Press, 1991), 371.

12. The usual requirements are given in para. 315.4a, 315.4b, and 315.6 of *The Book of Discipline, 2000*, 194. At minimum, it involves graduate theological study.

13. For a list of these schools (with mailing addresses and phone numbers) look at the *United Methodist Directory* (Nashville: Cokesbury, 2000), 201–11.

14. One modern-day effort to recapture the values and insights of the Church of the early centuries is a multivolume series, Thomas C. Oden, general editor, *Ancient Christian Commentary on Scripture* (Downers Grove, Ill.: InterVarsity Press). When completed, twenty-eight volumes will record biblical commentary from writers in the first seven centuries.

15. Isa. 30:6.

16. Deut. 6:20–21.

17. Ask your pastor to tell you the story about the woman who always trimmed the ham before she put it into the frying pan. Most preachers will know the story. Remember to be polite and laugh at the appropriate time.

18. Do you keep a diary? I have written in my journal every day for almost twenty years. I have the journal kept by my grandfather from 1895 until 1953. His

first entry says simply: "In Pantego, N.C., packing to move to Greenville, Pitt County, N.C." His final entry reads: "At home. 60 degrees at 7 A.M. 75 degrees at 5 P.M." What a story is told in between! It begins with a young pastor preparing to move to a new assignment and closes with an elderly man whose main activity is noting the temperature. These are precious documents for me.

19. *The Book of Discipline, 2000*, para. 104, 82.

20. It is a bit dangerous to start a list of such books. Let me mention just four: Peter Cartwright, *The Autobiography of Peter Cartwright* (Nashville: Abingdon Press, 1956); Arnold A. Daillimore, *Susanna Wesley: The Mother of John and Charles Wesley* (Grand Rapids: Baker Book House, 1993); Paul W. Milhouse, *Philip William Otterbein: Pioneer Pastor to Germans in America* (Nashville: Upper Room, 1968); Warren Thomas Smith, *Harry Hosier: Circuit Rider* (Nashville: Upper Room, 1981). This short list—too short!—includes a rough-speaking man who once ran against Abraham Lincoln for Congress, a remarkable mother who was a major influence on the ten of her nineteen children who lived to adulthood, a highly educated teacher who came to the United States because someone needed to spread the gospel among the many German-speaking people here, and an unlettered man of African descent who might well have been the best preacher of his day. Great stories of Christian experience!

CHAPTER 6. THE START

1. See Daniel T. Benedict, *Come to the Waters* (Nashville: Discipleship Resources, 1996). In this book, Dr. Benedict seeks to make baptism preparation and ritual fit the spiritual journey of the seeker, the one who is new to faith discovery.

2. Ted A. Campbell, *Methodist Doctrine* (Nashville: Abingdon Press, 1999), 72.

3. George Kohler is quoted in Weems, *John Wesley's Message Today* (83) as offering these six balancing acts in Methodist (Wesleyan) theology: faith and works; gospel and law; Scripture and experience; justification and sanctification; Word and sacraments; criticism of church and support of church. In each of these cases, traditional Methodist thinkers find a middle ground between extremes. For example, the basic service of worship in United Methodism is a service of *both* Word (preaching, Scripture) *and* Table (Holy Communion). See pages 2–31 in the *United Methodist Hymnal.*

4. *The Book of Discipline, 2000*, para. 103, article 6, 68.

5. Ibid.

6. Article 17 of the Articles of Religion of the former Methodist Church says

this of baptism: "Baptism is not only a sign of profession and mark of difference whereby Christians are distinguished from others that are not baptized; but it is also a sign of regeneration or the new birth. The Baptism of young children is to be retained in the Church." (*The Book of Discipline, 2000*, para. 103, article 17, 63.)

7. Outler, ed., *The Works of John Wesley*, vol. 1, 417.

8. Peter Cartwright was a Methodist circuit rider (preacher who went from place to place on horseback) in the first half of the nineteenth century. He felt strongly that it was wrong to require a person to be immersed for baptism. In his autobiography, he spoke of those who insisted on immersion as the only true baptism: "they made so much ado about baptism by immersion, that the uninformed would suppose that heaven was an island, and there was no way to get there but by diving or swimming" (Peter Cartwright, *The Autobiography of Peter Cartwright* [Nashville: Abingdon Press, 1956], 97).

9. The Holy Spirit is also called the Holy Ghost. Also Breath of Life. Also Root of Life. Also Wind. Also Breath of God. Also Comforter. Also Truth Divine. Also Sacred Fire. Also Spirit of Faith. Also Flame.

10. The Articles of Religion of the (former) Methodist Church state, "There is but one living and true God, everlasting, without body or parts, of infinite power, wisdom, and goodness; the maker and preserver of all things, both visible and invisible. And in unity of this Godhead there are three persons, of one substance, power, and eternity—the Father, the Son, and the Holy Ghost" (*The Book of Discipline, 2000*, para. 103, article 1, 59).

11. Justo González, *Mañana* (Nashville: Abingdon Press, 1990), 113.

12. Have you ever sung the hymn "Holy, Holy, Holy"? That hymn is a celebration of the Trinity. Note the name of the hymn tune (usually found at the bottom or top of the page with the words): "Nicaea." The music gets its name from Nicaea, where the teaching about the Trinity was so strongly defended. Now that you know this, you might consider using this information in a church trivia contest.

13. If you can put your hands on *The United Methodist Hymnal*, check out hymn 105: "God of Many Names." Look at the fourth stanza of hymn 139: "Then to thy need God as a mother doth speed, spreading the wings of grace o'er thee." Other examples of introducing a variety of names for God can be found in *The Faith We Sing* (Nashville: Abingdon Press, 2000), a supplement to the *United Methodist Hymnal*. For that book, Ruth Duck has written (hymn 2046) "Mother, Brother, Holy Partner, Father, Spirit, Only Son" ("Womb of Life," copyright © 1992 by GIA Publications, Inc., Chicago, Illinois. All rights reserved. Used by permission); Brian Wren has offered (hymn 2047) "Strong mother God, working

night and day . . ." (Copyright © 1989, 1944, Hope Publishing Company. Used with permission); Jean Janzen starts a hymn (hymn 2050), "Mothering God . . ." (Words by Jean Janzen, based on the writings of Juliana of Norwich [fifteenth century], copyright 1991, Abingdon Press, administered by The Copyright Company, Nashville, TN from *The Faith We Sing*, published by Abingdon Press). These hymns remind us that images of God are both masculine and feminine and that none is adequate to capture all of Who God is!

CHAPTER 7. THE MEANS

1. Sadly, this reminds me of a story. A driver locked the keys to the car in the car with the engine running. Calling a towing service for help, the driver was asked to identify the car so the helper truck could find the vehicle. "You won't have any trouble spotting me," the driver said. "I am on Broad Street; the car is a red convertible with the top down." No comment.

2. John Wesley preached this sermon to correct a view he sometimes called "quietism." Persons who advocated "quietism" argued that all a Christian had to do to receive God's grace was to wait for God to deliver it. Wesley argued that the grace was indeed God's to give as God chose but that God had established ways to give such grace and Christians would do well to employ those ordinary means of grace. It was a typical Wesleyan balance between two extremes: God's action and human activity.

3. Outler, ed., *The Works of John Wesley*, vol. 1, 381.

4. *The Book of Discipline, 2000*, para. 103, 72–74. The Constitution of the United Methodist Church prohibits changing these General Rules (*The Book of Discipline, 2000*, para. 19, 27).

5. Ibid., para. 103, 74.

6. Outler, ed., *The Works of John Wesley*, vol. 1, 382.

7. One place Joyce might have looked is Rom. 6:1–2: "What then are we to say? Should we continue in sin in order that grace may abound? By no means! How can we who have died to sin go on living in it?"

8. A good place to read about the various Christian views of the Lord's Supper is Rob L. Staples's, *Outward Sign and Inward Grace: The Place of Sacraments in Wesleyan Spirituality* (Kansas City: Beacon Hill Press, 1991), 211–28.

9. The resolution reads, "Whereas, it has been our practice for two centuries to use what the ritual printed in our hymnals has referred to as 'the pure, unfermented juice of the grape' for Holy Communion; and whereas, this terminology was inadvertently omitted when the present hymnal was adopted; therefore, be it resolved,

that the 1996 General Conference restore this phrase to our ritual by ordering that the words 'The pure, unfermented juice of the grape shall be used during the service of Holy Communion' be added beneath the headings 'A Service of Word and Table I,' 'A Service of Word and Table II,' and 'A Service of Word and Table III.'" (*The Book of Resolutions of The United Methodist Church, 1996* [Nashville: United Methodist Publishing House, 1996], 838.)

10. The Constitution of the United Methodist Church has recently been amended to read, "The United Methodist Church is a part of the church universal, which is one Body in Christ. The United Methodist Church acknowledges that all persons are of sacred worth. All persons, without regard to race, color, national origin, status, or economic condition, shall be eligible to attend its worship services, participate in its programs, *receive the sacraments*, upon baptism be admitted as baptized members, and upon taking vows declaring the Christian faith, become professing members in any local church in the connection." (Italics added. Approved by 2000 General Conference, ratified by annual conferences' vote, declared by Council of Bishops.)

11. Read about this period in Lester Ruth, *A Little Heaven Below* (Nashville: Kingswood Books, an imprint of Abingdon Press, 2000), 125–31.

12. Henry D. Rack, *Reasonable Enthusiast* (Philadelphia: Trinity Press International, 1989), 405–7.

13. *United Methodist Hymnal*, 12.

14. Most books on John Wesley speak of this custom; for example, look at Rack, *Reasonable Enthusiast*, 403.

15. A United Methodist News Service release on January 31, 2002, gives a preliminary report from the committee studying Holy Communion for the United Methodist Church: "The committee affirmed that idea (weekly Communion) in a working statement that it adopted: 'Out of faithfulness to the Sunday worship encouraged by John Wesley and the wider tradition of the Church, and believing that our United Methodist worship life and fellowship will be enriched as we live into weekly celebration of the Lord's Supper on the Lord's Day, the Holy Communion Study Committee affirms the value of The United Methodist Church moving towards a richer sacramental life, including weekly celebration of the Lord's Supper as advocated by the general orders of Sunday worship in our United Methodist hymnals and book of worship, while recognizing that not every service will include Holy Communion." (If the 2004 General Conference accepts this report, it comes as an encouragement, not a mandate, for weekly Communion.)

16. *The United Methodist Book of Worship*, 115.

17. *The United Methodist Book of Worship* offers help for those who bring Holy Communion to homebound or hospitalized persons (see p. 51).

18. *The Book of Discipline, 2000*, 62.

19. Matt. 18:20.

20. *The Book of Discipline, 2000*, para. 103, article 22, 65.

21. "Whosoever, through his private judgment, willingly and purposely doth openly break the rites and ceremonies of the church to which he belongs, which are not repugnant to the Word of God, and are ordained and approved by common authority, ought to be rebuked openly." (Ibid.)

22. John 17:21.

23. Rev. 5:11.

24. If you want to learn more about how Methodists around the world worship, read *The Sunday Service of the Methodists*, ed. Karen B. Westerfield Tucker (Nashville: Kingswood Books, an imprint of Abingdon Press, 1996). This book looks at contemporary, traditional, liturgical, free-form worship with Methodist heritage around the world.

25. Outler, ed., *The Works of John Wesley*, vol. 1, 575.

26. Ibid., 577.

27. Marjorie Suchocki, "The Perfection of Prayer," in Randy L. Maddox, ed., *Rethinking Wesley's Theology for Contemporary Methodism* (Nashville: Kingswood Books, an imprint of Abingdon Press, 1998), 53.

28. Mark 14:36; John 5:30; Luke 22:42; Matt. 26:39.

29. *The United Methodist Book of Worship* and *The United Methodist Hymnal* are filled with examples of such prayers.

30. Our friend Wallace Kirby has taught Toni and me a prayer discipline we use at supper each evening. We take the Christmas cards received during the previous year and each evening take one of those cards and pray for the person or persons who sent it.

31. *The Book of Discipline, 2000*, para. 321, 204; para. 328, 214.

32. Outler, ed., *The Works of John Wesley*, vol. 1, 597–601.

33. Campbell, *Methodist Doctrine*, 87.

34. John Wesley's sermon "Causes of the Inefficacy of Christianity" is quoted in Reuben Job, *A Wesleyan Spiritual Reader* (Nashville: Abingdon Press, 1997), 27.

CHAPTER 8. THE DOING

1. Outler, ed., *The Works of John Wesley*, vol. 1, 533.

2. Quoted in Weems, *John Wesley's Message Today*, 62, from an introduction to "The Poetical Works of John Wesley and Charles Wesley."

3. The first *Book of Discipline, 1785* uses a question-and-answer format: "Q.: What may we reasonably believe to be God's Design in raising up the Preachers called Methodists? A.: To reform the Continent, and to spread scriptural holiness over these Lands." Russell E. Richey, Kenneth E. Rowe, and Jean Miller Schmidt, eds., *The Methodist Experience in America: A Sourcebook*, vol. 2 (Nashville: Abingdon Press, 2000), 82.

4. This list is suggested by Weems, *John Wesley's Message Today,* 64–70.

5. *The Book of Discipline, 2000*, part 4, 95.

6. Topics include Water, Air, Soil, Minerals, Plants; Energy Resources Utilization; Animal Life; Space; Science and Technology; Food Safety; The Family; Other Christian Communities; Marriage; Divorce; Single Persons; Women and Men; Human Sexuality; Family Violence and Abuse; Sexual Harassment; Abortion; Adoption; Faithful Care of the Dying; Suicide; Rights of Racial and Ethnic Persons; Racism; Rights of Religious Minorities; Rights of Children; Rights of Young People; Rights of the Aging; Rights of Women; Rights of Persons with Disabilities; Equal Rights Regardless of Sexual Orientation; Population; Alcohol and Other Drugs; Tobacco; Medical Experimentation; Genetic Technology; Rural Life; Sustainable Agriculture; Urban-Suburban Life; Media Violence and Christian Values; The Internet; Persons Living with HIV and AIDS; Right to Health Care; Organ Transplantation and Donation; Property; Collective Bargaining; Work and Leisure; Consumption; Poverty; Migrant Workers; Gambling; Family Farms; Corporate Responsibility; Basic Freedoms and Human Rights; Political Responsibility; Freedom of Information; Education; Civil Obedience and Civil Disobedience; Criminal and Restorative Justice; Military Service; Nations and Cultures; National Power and Responsibility; War and Peace; and Justice and Law. If you want more information on any of these topics, look in *The Book of Discipline, 2000*, 95–122.

7. Col. 1:18–20.

8. Outler, ed., *The Works of John Wesley*, vol. 2, 99–105.

9. Matt. 5:48.

10. Luke 10:27.

11. *The Book of Discipline, 2000*, para. 321, 204; para. 327, 214.

12. Galatians 2:20.

13. Hymn "Love Divine, All Loves Excelling," *United Methodist Hymnal*, 384.

14. *The Book of Discipline, 2000*, para. 101, 47.

15. W. Reginald Ward and Richard P. Heitzenrater, eds., *The Works of John Wesley*, vol. 18, 249–50. (Methodists refer to this account as Wesley's Aldersgate experience. Some congregations are named Aldersgate Church.)

16. Campbell, *Methodist Doctrine*, 57.

17. *United Methodist Hymnal*, 369.

18. Quoted in Weems, *John Wesley's Message Today*, 38.

CHAPTER 9. THE WAY

1. *The Book of Discipline, 2000*, para. 215, 130. ["A member of any local United Methodist church is a member of the denomination and the catholic (universal) church."]

2. Ibid., para. 130, 90.

3. Look back at chapter 3, "The People." Some of the biblical roots mentioned there are Gen. 2:18; Exod. 14–15; 31:18; 32:15; Neh. 9:38–10:26; Matt. 4:18–22; 10:1–4; Acts 2:42–44; 2:1; 9:17–19; 15:2; 1 Cor. 8:19; Eph. 2:19; Heb. 12:1; James 5:16; Rev. 7:9; 21:2.

4. This statement was in a letter Wesley wrote in 1746 to John Smith, quoted in Thomas Edward Frank, *Polity, Practice, and the Mission of The United Methodist Church* (Nashville: Abingdon Press, 2002), 42.

5. How many Methodists does it take to change a lightbulb? I don't know; the committee has not given its report yet.

6. *The Book of Discipline, 2000*, para. 245, 145.

7. Ibid., para. 331.3, 220.

8. Ibid., para. 417, 282; para. 415.4, 281.

9. Ibid., para. 25.4, 29; para. 601, 331.

10. Ibid., para. 365.1, 263.

11. Ibid., para. 407, 271.

12. Ibid., para. 35, 33.

13. Ibid., para. 36, 33.

14. Ibid., para. 406, 270.

15. Ibid., para. 15, 25–27.

16. Ibid., para. 16–20, 27.

17. Quoted in Russell E. Richey, *The Methodist Conference in America* (Nashville: Kingswood Books, an imprint of Abingdon Press, 1996), 15.

18. Ibid., 16.

19. If you like to spend quiet evenings reading about church structure, grab a copy of *The Book of Discipline, 2000* and pour over paragraphs 501–510 (General Conference), paragraphs 401–416 (bishops), and paragraphs 2601–2612 (Judicial Council).

20. *The Book of Discipline, 2000*, para. 431, 290.

21. John Wesley, *Explanatory Notes upon the New Testament*, 478–79, comments on Acts 20:28: "No man or number of men upon earth can constitute an overseer, bishop, or any other Christian minister. To do this is the peculiar work of the Holy Ghost."

22. Quoted in Richard Heitzenrater, "Connectionalism and Itinerancy," in Russell E. Richey, Dennis M. Campbell, and William B. Lawrence, eds., *Connectionalism: Ecclesiology, Mission, and Identity* (Nashville: Abingdon Press, 1997), 33.

23. *The Book of Discipline, 2000*, para. 319, 209.

24. Ibid., para. 323, 200.

25. Ibid., para. 340–43, 231–35.

26. Wesley, *Explanatory Notes upon the New Testament*, 618.

27. If you want to dig further into biblical teachings about the role of women in the faith community, a good resource is Carol A. Newsom and Sharon H. Ringe, eds., *The Women's Bible Commentary* (Louisville, Ky.: Westminster/John Knox Press, 1992).

28. Wesley, *Explanatory Notes upon the New Testament*, 619.

29. The energy with which United Methodists debate issues related to homosexuality suggests that many view this as an essential issue. For example, the General Conference has voted several times to prohibit the ordination of self-avowed, practicing homosexual persons. Each time, however, about one-third of those voting wanted to remove the prohibition. On nonessential matters, a vote is taken, a consensus is formed, and life moves on. On essential matters, however, persons have a greater investment in the outcome. The issue does not go away until the leading of God's Spirit becomes clearer. If one-third of those who faithfully seek God's leading come to a conclusion different from the majority, it makes me think that we have not yet heard all God wants to say to us.

30. *The Book of Discipline, 2000*, para. 2501, 649.

31. Ibid., para. 2503.1, 650.

32. Ibid., 21–39.

CHAPTER 10. THE OTHERS

1. *United Methodist Hymnal*, 880–882.

2. John 14:6.

3. John 10:16.

4. *The Book of Discipline, 2000*, para. 101, 43–44.

5. *The Book of Discipline, 2000*, para. 2404, 646–48.

6. Wesley, *Explanatory Notes upon the New Testament*, 375.

7. Outler, ed., *The Works of John Wesley*, vol. 2, 94.

8. Quoted in John B. Cobb Jr., *Grace and Responsibility: A Wesleyan Theology for Today* (Nashville: Abingdon Press, 1995), 146.

9. *The Book of Discipline, 2000*, para. 1902.2, 627.

10. M. Thomas Thangaraj, a Christian who grew up in a predominantly non-Christian culture, has written of several approaches to relating to persons of other religions: (a) We know and they know not; (b) We perhaps know; they perhaps know. Who knows? (c) What we have is good for us; what they have is good for them; (d) We know in full; they know in part; (e) We know and know that we know; they know and know not that they know; (f) We and they together need to know more! (Thangaraj, *Relating to People of Other Religions: What Every Christian Should Know* [Nashville: Abingdon Press, 1997]). Do you recognize yourself in any of these approaches? Dr. Thangaraj invites Christians to make a witness that has gentleness and reverence.

11. *The Book of Resolutions of The United Methodist Church, 2000* (Nashville: United Methodist Publishing House, 2000), 194.

12. Ibid., 746.

13. *The Book of Discipline, 2000*, para. 162, 105.

14. Quoted in Cobb, *Grace and Responsibility: A Wesleyan Theology for Today,* 147.

15. Wesley, *Explanatory Notes upon the New Testament*, 435.

16. *The United Methodist Hymnal*, 332.